THE CASE IS ALTERED

About the Author

The author is a former high profile Senior Civil Servant and Past President of a leading international chartered professional body. He holds a PhD, from the University of Loughborough in Human and Environmental Studies. He was awarded an Honorary Fellowship by Bath Spa University for his outstanding contribution to the development of British Higher Education. He has publications in this field and a book and numerous published papers in the Christian field. He is also an Associate of The Michaelis Guild of the Froebel Institute (University of London at Roehampton) and a former governor. After active service in The Royal Navy he was responsible for administration in a leading London Medical School for ten years. He then served in the British Overseas Civil Service in West Africa as a principal. He subsequently joined the home Civil Service holding posts in the Department of Trade and Industry and the Department of Education and Science. He was married to Ruth for fifty-seven years until she died in 2009. He has one son, one grandson and two great granddaughters. He has been involved as an advisor to Lifeword, the Christian Service Training Council, the Open Theological College, the Centre for British Teachers and as an honorary lecturer at Redcliff Missionary Training College.

THE CASE IS ALTERED

WOMEN IN CHURCH, RELIGION & SOCIETY

V J DELANY

EDOCEO PUBLICATIONS

First published in 2011 by Edoceo Publications
64 Third Avenue, Frinton-On-Sea, Essex, CO13 9EE
www.amolibros.co.uk

Distributed by Gardners Books, 1 Whittle Drive, Eastbourne, East Sussex, BN23 6QH
Tel: +44(0)1323 521555 | Fax: +44(0)1323 521666

British Library Cataloguing in Publication Data
A catalogue record for this book is available from the British Library.

ISBN 978-0-9559003-1-0

Typeset by Amolibros, Milverton, Somerset
This book production has been managed by Amolibros
www.amolibros.com
Printed and bound by T J International Ltd, Padstow, Cornwall, UK

Contents

PREFACE

"...quickly state; all equal are within the Church's gate". *The Church Porch: George Herbert. 1593-1633.*

Prove all Things

A powerful case has been built up by men from the beginning of time against allowing women to enjoy spiritual parity. Yet on serious reflection it is hard to reconcile this with the nature of an impartial God. When things are not what they seem to be easy-going people are all too ready to take appearances at face value. It is refreshing however whenever a person is prepared to scrutinize an unclear situation in order to get a better explanation. I began to write this book as a study of discovery as to why women are seriously discriminated against in the Christian Church, and, apparently, how far their treatment has deviated from what God intended. The treatment of women in society has never been totally fair. Men have, largely, regarded women as subservient. In spite of this, there has been a steady progression in feminine emancipation in democratic countries. Yet this pace has not been matched in the Church because in its circles discussions about change have proved much more protracted and contentious.

In looking at why there has always been prejudice against women I identified a number of circumstances in religion and in society that have contributed to this problem. These range from aspects of tradition, tribalism, and culture, to custom and physiological difference. I must make it clear to readers from the outset that although criticizing the adverse affect of these aspects upon the position of women, I am also conscious of the value of organized institutions in protecting people in a corporate sense throughout history. Whoever or whatever I take to task as being responsible for the subjugation of women should not necessarily be condemned as having no merit.

I am confident that virtually everyone who is sympathetic towards my case for the advancement of women's rights in the Church will go along with my contentions. However, eyebrows may well be raised by my identification of the traditionalist view of priests as a stumbling block. But this does not mean that those so labelled have no calling. Care must be taken over semantics. The adoption of one title does not necessarily mean that an individual cannot at the same time be endowed with a ministry gift of the Holy Spirit. In fact by my understanding of the Bible, as will emerge, all true believers are kings and priests to God. There are not two classes of Christian.

I am unsure what readers will make of the boldness I have shown in Part III in which I speculate about changes in worship that might be brought about if women are given equal rights in ministry. My thoughts are exploratory and should be seen as such. I have left some of these as questions still to be answered.

Altering the Case

I have taken the title of my book, *The Case is Altered*, from the name of an inn at Wealdstone in Middlesex. It stands opposite a court house. A story goes that a case was inconclusive after a morning session. The judiciary adjourned, piecemeal, to the hostelry for a good lunch and then, being in a more congenial frame of mind and having discussed things informally, the case was altered in the afternoon session. I am going to use this local yarn as an illustration by applying it to an alteration of attitude on my part, and then to the current debate about woman's rightful position in the Christian Church. I am also going to describe the differences there have been between attitudes of religionists towards women in the Church and those who have influenced society, culture, and custom.

Firstly, in an original draft of this book I failed to make my main argument clear enough. I was obscuring the main thrust of my argument. I got wound up about the manner in which women were being treated and in consequence some of my opinions were too partisan. I rushed a manuscript out in two months, and what was meant to be a case for parity based on the impartiality of God, turned out to be clouded by personal prejudice. In retrospect I saw that I had not got the best balance. I had intended my book to be a model of fair thinking and that was not how it had turned out. The court story is appealing. Just imagine how the afternoon proceedings at Wealdstone might have changed from the indecisive and one-sided arguments of the morning session to a learned and measured debate in the afternoon followed by an intelligent weighing up. I am now basing my case for the rights of women by linking it with this legendary local court fable.

Firstly, a leading publisher enjoyed reading my manuscript but fortunately decided not to proceed with publication. Along with two other "promising submissions", it became a victim of the present turbulence in the publishing industry. I was, mercifully, given breathing space to alter my case. There is a lesson here not for myself only but also for all those who are too partisan.

Secondly, in the wider debate about women's rights, advocates of continued male supremacy are not, currently, being challenged effectively. While they robustly argue their case, those who think otherwise are not always finding ways of debating the issue publicly. Each side is simply going its own way. Better ways need to be found of getting diehards to change tack, and of convincing the ambivalent. There has been debate in the Synod of the Church of England but each side still maintains an entrenched position. That is why, in order to break this impasse, I am likening the current situation to the forenoon proceedings of the court at Wealdstone. These consist of each side, the prosecution and the defence, making separate submissions. By the midday adjournment no counter arguments, or summing up would have been made, and no verdict delivered.

A morning session at assizes is adorned with wigs and gowns. There is protocol, strict law, and prissiness. However, at lunchtime there is opportunity for reflection; people talk one to one. Counsels mull over each other's submissions. The judge has a good lunch. The afternoon proceedings are different. Counsels seek to demolish respectively their rivals' morning arguments. The judge sums up with erudition, showing knowledge of equity and retrieving precedents from legal sources. A more relaxed jury benefits from the way the proceedings are developing. It is less influenced by what it read or heard previously or by the appearance of the defendant. The case is altered.

Making my Case

Less us imagine there is a great court case providing an opportunity to unravel reasons why women have always been treated so unequally. It will hear a counter argument against the entrenched views of influential men, and sadly to say, collectively of a number of denominations. I am the one who is the advocate of the case for women. I am showing that the denigrators of women have been mistaken, and that they are not declaring a self-interest. Their intransigence needs to be countered with sound theological reasoning, and logical argument based upon lateral thinking. I am taking commonly supposed meanings of key scriptures and showing how these are taken out of context by men and how they sideline other relevant verses. I trust this will help those who up until now have depended upon an innate sense of justice alone to support the feminine cause. In order to flesh out a fascinating and topical debate I am including comparisons, drawn from a long and painful history of the treatment of women in secular society and from these studies I also learned a remarkable lesson from contemporary religion. In addition to showing that a number of theological arguments in support of the superiority of men depends upon conveniently selected scriptures, I am pointing out the way the authority of scripture has been undermined by the introduction and equal ranking of the traditions of men. Jesus was in headlong conflict with religious leaders because he opposed tradition whenever this was contrary to his divine mind. He also claimed that they erred because they did not know the scriptures or the power of God. I will show later that most of the early Church fathers were adamant about the dangers of importing tradition into doctrinal teaching. The proponents of orthodoxy developed its complex system by reliance upon tradition. This is not generally recognized. My case for the liberation of women will rest heavily upon this fact.

It is not surprising to find the doctrines that obliged women to keep silent in church and forbade them to teach or usurp authority over men were introduced partly by taking scriptures out of context, partly by reliance upon tradition, and partly by ignoring other scriptures. Conjectures about the significance of Jesus only calling men are circumstantial, and convenient to the masculine case. This I will show by presenting material that will convince impartial readers that this case is flawed.

The road to Christian maturity is long and arduous: a path upon which God strives to bring rebellious creatures back to Himself. Mankind is entirely responsible for its poor rate of spiritual progress and God does not force people to do things against their will. Those who believe that He does so, completely misunderstand the divine nature.

A Trap

I realized that I was wrong to condemn the evil actions of men in my original manuscript just because they were men and equally wrong to praise the good actions of women just because they were women. I fell into a trap. After rightly and indignantly condemning the behaviour of paedophile Irish priests, following the damning official report about them, I asserted that a woman bishop would not perpetrate such crimes, and that if priests were allowed to marry, their wives would be a restraining influence. Not long afterwards the Vanessa George case emerged: the woman who abused children under her care at a nursery. This was followed by disclosures of cases in which large numbers of women had been convicted of abusing their own children. The lesson I learnt was that evil men and evil women are evil because they are fallen creatures and not because of their gender. Conversely, good men and good women are good because they are spiritually "in Christ" and not because of their gender. The Apostle Paul enjoined all people to examine themselves to see whether they were in the faith. They would be aware that Christ was in them except they were reprobates. Gender did not enter into his spiritual equation. It can be seen that it does not matter whether one is a man or a women, a Catholic, Anglican, Baptist, Methodist, or a Pentecostal. The test of acceptance by God is of being a new creature or not. It has nothing to do with denomination, tradition, custom or any such thing.

One New Person

The Apostle Paul, when known as Saul, a Pharisee, and under the law, held views that dramatically altered upon the Damascus Road. He was not afraid to admit it. Before his enlightenment he found reasons to justify his stance (as opinionated persons do today). He was circumcised on the eighth day, of the tribe of Benjamin, a Hebrew of the Hebrews, in regard to the law a Pharisee, as for zeal persecuting the Church, as to legalist righteousness, faultless. Yet afterwards he counted all these things as loss (or as nothing or as rubbish) by comparison with being found as "in Christ". He reckoned that neither circumcision nor uncircumcision meant anything. What counted was a new creation. In other words being a Gentile or being a Jew, being under the law, or being outside of it, was immaterial. In another place Paul put this differently. He wrote that there is neither Jew nor Greek, there is neither bond nor free, there is neither male nor female for all are one in Christ.

A Caveat

I am familiar with the case that is contrary to mine. It is based upon interpretations of scripture and upon tradition: giving each equal weight. I acknowledge this is sometimes sincerely held and, therefore, I do not intend to contemn its proponents as individuals. I, personally, do not believe that tradition merits equal weight with scripture and will show that tradition often contradicts scripture or is not supported by it. I am following the dictum that the Spirit of God and the Word of God must agree. My intention is to describe practices from which women are excluded and to demonstrate how much better it would be if there was a level playing field.

My Purpose

All that I have learned and understood about the nature of a holy God during a long life has convinced me of His complete impartiality. It saddens me that men prefer to adopt the mores of tradition and custom rather than to follow that which is spiritual and thereby exclude women from participating fully in worship and service.

I am addressing, primarily, the question of the rightful role of women in the Christian Church. By and large women are still being denied equal opportunities for exercising ministry in both worship and service. In presenting an argument against the subjection of women I am including reviews of their place in society, and also contrasting attitudes towards them in religion generally and in culture. My conclusions are that, potentially, equality could be introduced quicker in the Christian Church than is possible in society, but to realists my view must appear anachronistic, because actual trends show just the reverse. This, of course, is a broad-brush statement based upon the history of western capitalist culture. The lot of women in some other cultures has not improved as significantly but in the youngest major world religion women have been equal from its inception in the sixteenth century. A further exception is the complete acceptance of women in ministry by some Christian denominations.

A Cause Célèbre

I had two brothers and two sisters as siblings. As a boy, my education was always co-educational. These experiences must have helped me in later life because I became completely impartial as to the sexes, when employing, working for, or electing people. In secular life I served in a senior capacity under a brilliant woman who went on to become the first woman British Prime Minister. On occasions, I also escorted her to and from church. I was an advisor for eight years to a woman academic who became a dame, Vice Chancellor of a university, was a member of the Equal Opportunities Commission and on the Synod of the Church of England. I was a governor of a leading university college whose lady principal was Pro-Chancellor of the university. I advised another woman Secretary of State, and held policy discussions about mathematical models with a double dame who was Lord Mayor of Manchester and Chancellor of the University of Salford.

Even subconsciously, I would help and encourage women and men on my staff without discrimination. Because of the exercise of gross inequality around me, I began actively promoting the advancement of women to such an extent that my motivation became something of a *cause célèbre*. A leading chartered professional body of which I became the international president boasted its 2,000th woman member in 1984. Currently it has 23,190 women out of a total roll of 78,000. At a presidential dinner I had a record number of women guests, including, on either side of me, a lady minister of state with a distinguished career in local government, later a dame, and the lady Senior Chief Inspector of Schools who later became Principal of Newnham College, Cambridge. I was proud that several years after I passed the chair we had a first lady president, who was a Nigerian, a director of British Telecom who was subsequently honored by Her Majesty the Queen.

I was married to a very supportive and trusting wife for fifty-seven years who died in January of last year. She had been a bomber crash ambulance driver in the WAAF's in WW2, and the younger of my two sisters was an ATS sergeant predictor operator in an anti-aircraft battery during the Blitz on Liverpool. On the subject of trust, and the double dame I have referred to: on one occasion I discussed mathematics for some hours with her. The following day an open card from her fell on my home doormat. It read: "Didn't we have fun yesterday – Kathleen!"

Readers will understand how, with a background like this, my original manuscript turned out to be rather prejudicial!

A One Man Campaign

As I disclosed in my recent publication *The Finger of God*, I am a committed Christian with a background that began in orthodoxy and continued in Bible-based evangelical Christianity. I still have friends across a whole spectrum of denominations (and indeed other faiths). I have been supplied with invaluable information about the Sikh religion by a highly informed lady of that faith. It forms the backbone of the thirteenth chapter.

Women have, generally, been self-effacing when it came to advocacy in their own cause, which is to their credit, though not to their advantage. I realized that one way of furthering the cause of women in the Church would be for a man to raise his head above the parapet and speak out on their behalf. When I told my niece about my intentions she pondered before commenting that, after all, half the people in the world must be women.

In order to understand something of the mystery of Godliness one needs to think laterally. At times it is difficult, with our finite minds, to fathom God's purposes, to comprehend his love for humanity, or to understand what he has prepared for those who love him in return. For instance, many are stumbled by an isolated sentence contained in a pastoral letter to an early Church without thinking laterally about the broader weight of scripture. I have a burden to show, that in His nature, God is impartial as to gender. I am making a biblical case for the complete emancipation of women in the Christian church. I believe that women are equal with men and that the way to turn such a right into reality is to relegate religious tradition and to steer a path leading to total spiritual liberty for all by the adoption of principles of impartiality.

The God Factor

In the beginning God intended a woman to be a man's companion. This would suggest that although she was different physiologically there was no reason for her to be subservient or that a man should be more privileged. Men have placed great store upon the fact that Eve came from Adam's rib but the Bible balances this up by stating that every man is born of a woman. Mankind's fallen nature exudes selfishness and a desire to dominate. This is why it was not easy after the fall, for God to re-establish communion with marred people whose origin was his handiwork. He started by telling Abraham to leave his home and people, and obediently Abraham responded by going in faith, not knowing where he was going. He was looking for a city whose architect and builder was God. It has been, and will continue to be, a long journey for mankind until God's perfection and righteousness are universally acknowledged. In the meantime there will be a tension between the divine fact of God's impartiality and a male inclination of selfishness. The prospects for women of enjoying rapid recognition are not good because the status quo is heavily loaded with traditional attitudes and influenced by male-dominated worldwide cultures.

In my view, the only acceptable way to tackle the present situation in the Church is to convince a majority of men, conclusively, that the Holy Bible shows that God is impartial. All other ways are pointless. For instance, it has been argued that the Church should accommodate itself to present-day worldly culture in which, steadily, women are making up ground. This would be dangerous: it would open the gates to an influx of other-worldly practices. For instance, present-day attitudes towards marriage and singleness do not conform to biblical teaching.

My adopted course has led me to trace God's path of reconciliation starting with Abraham, and continuing with the history and laws of a chosen nation; its rejection of a Messiah; and the emergence of that Messiah as a potential deliverer of everybody. Although, as in the case of Abraham, people did not, until the fullness of time, completely understand the nature of God's intended outcome, it is now possible to look back and marvel at the extraordinary workings of the divine chronometer. The ceremonies and feasts of ancient Israel are now obsolete but served to point me to the extraordinary portents these foreshadowed. Instead of being pointless and boring, instead of being a system that cried out for modification, these were events and practices that foreshadowed the emergence of a completely new and glorious spiritual freedom in Christ. This was to be a freedom for all, regardless of race or gender. In God's estimate such freedom exists now. But, because of a divine willingness to permit free will, enjoyment of his munificence is marred by male self-interests. It is, invariably, dangerous when holders of power can lay down their own agendas. A person or groups of people, with absolute power can become in attitude very self-opinionated.

Contrary Views

There are, of course, many who hold genuinely different views about the rights of women to be elders (or bishops) and these rely heavily on Paul's comments in letters addressed to apostolic churches. These also claim that passages in both Peter and Paul have been rightly translated in modern versions that treat the Greek word *kephale* as meaning "head" and not "source" as in ordinary Greek usage. I answer their arguments in Chapter Five, in which I contend that they overlook that the early Church was subject to the tradition and culture of the day in which a man was the head of the family, and they ignore all the other scriptures that refer to the spiritual equality of all in Christ. I also address arguments that seek the separation of worth from power in order to leave women with inferior rights. Authority and power are virtually synonymous in the light of the Great Commission and the enduement of power at Pentecost.

I will show that many former religious ceremonies and offices have been perpetuated needlessly, and that these are all male-dominated. Sadly, such actions have been detrimental to the freedom of women in the Church. I am not suggesting that some denominations are obsolete as such, but, simply, that there is a need for substantial reform from within, involving repentance, and a change of attitude towards women. There are other differences and schisms involving all sorts of issues in the broad Church. Readers should note that I do not go into these, except when, and only when, these impinge on the subject of the inferior role of women.

I mention here that it is anomalous when a single scripture is given great weight to support a case against the authority of women by people who disregard numerous other scriptures or rely solely on tradition when developing doctrines. The semantics of religion are littered with key words that do not figure in the Bible at all. For example: "eucharist", "sacrament", "saint" (as opposed to "saved one"), are words that have been introduced by orthodox theologians. Eucharistic theology did not figure in the first 1,000 years of the Church.

The Roman rite identifies seven sacraments whereas Luther and exponents of "reformed doctrine" acknowledge two: baptism and the Lord's Table. The bible rates these more as simple commands and not as religious ordinances. "Sacraments" have spiritual connotations, and until quite recently women were not permitted to administer any of these and they are still completely banned from doing so in certain large denominations.

Counter Argument

I address a number of other arguments that are made by men to justify their supremacy. I show that, invariably, men disregard explanations other than their own. As an instance, it is argued that because Jesus only called men as his first followers this is a norm to be followed for all time. My counter argument is that it would have been completely improper in his day for Jesus, an unmarried man, to invite women to follow him. Many women followed him voluntarily and he was glad of their physical and financial support as he went through all the towns and villages. In Chapters Two, Three, and Four, especially, I show how many women helped Jesus and generally how women have been greatly used by God down the ages.

Then and Now

When authentic Christians die they are received by their Lord. It is absurd to suggest that sex, denomination, or religious status will count for anything in such an eventuality. Nothing will count but a new creature. So, why on earth do men continue to discriminate against women? It is most likely that it is borne of a desire to dominate. If so, it is a desire of their old nature, and this is a trait which will have to be accounted for either on the Day of Judgment, or else resolved in accordance with God's will on earth. Thy will by done on earth as it is heaven! On the day of the Lord and forever afterwards those who reign with him will not be exclusively men. Any pecking order will be determined by our impartial and Holy God.

God does not Change

Although earthly customs, traditions, and cultures change with the passing of time, the Father God never changes neither does his Son. Jesus Christ is the same, yesterday, today and forever. God may have condoned, tolerated, or winked at man's inability to match up with heavenly standards in the past but he never came down to mortal standards himself. It is a powerful part of my argument that an unchanging God cannot be impartial in one moment of time and be happy to discriminate against women at another. On a divine plane only the things of the spirit reign – and where the spirit is there is liberty.

Acknowledgments

I dedicate this book to that half of the world's population who are women, and particularly to the baronesses, dames, and ladies referred to in the Preface. (They are listed later.) Thanks are due to Gurcharan Morgan for telling me so much about Sikhism, to Rev Ben Marlowe for custodianship of chapters, and to Rebecca Burnett, and Mark Betteridge for computer work.

PART ONE

BIBLICAL AUTHORITY

Chapter One

SPIRITUAL EQUALITY

"What counts is a new creation." Galatians 6:15

It is in God's very nature to treat everybody the same. Unfortunately, however, our frail human nature is such that it means we are not always as impartial as is our creator.

A dim view of God

Men in the Christian Church are not, normally, women-haters. Our problem is that some of us appear to think that God has a down on the fairer sex. Whether we really think this or not is conjectural. It is more than likely, judging from history, that men fabricated a nature for God that would suit their own ends. Whatever their motives may have been, it is my intention to refute, passionately, any innuendo that paints God as a misogynist. I will show that scripture reveals that women are in no way inferior or under-privileged in the eyes of the Holy Spirit. I will then go on to show how antagonists quote scriptures in selective and limited ways; include tradition, and take advantage of inertia brought about by cultures and taboos. Yes, men conspired to prevent women from getting a look-in when it came to opportunities for ministry. Gradually and fortuitously, and with support of enlightened men, women were allowed to come, by stages, into their own. This was not the case in certain major denominations and in some others progress has been slow. The Salvation Army and most Pentecostal denominations do not discriminate against women. The Methodist Church is also very open and has many new female ministers.

In Christ one's sex is irrelevant

God is so ambivalent about gender that His word does not fuss about the subject. For the most part it takes the equality of all for granted. Those who oppose the ministry of women in the Church are blind to the significance of the use of the word "all": a word that is commonly used in the Bible to address everyone. The reason why Jesus said so little on the subject of the respective status of the sexes was that biological differences are irrelevant in a new creation. It should also be noted that the term "man" is all-embracing. Some modern translations prefer to use "people".

Women are "Sons of God"

Some verses written by the Apostle Paul are used by teachers of male supremacy to deprive women from following a genuine calling to serve equally with them in the Church. Verses found in his letters to Timothy, dealt with in detail later, are taken out of their context and presented in isolation. Yet Paul has provided us with unequivocal teaching elsewhere about the equality of *all* in Christ. In his letter to the Galatians he wrote that *all* are Sons of God by faith in Christ Jesus and he gave a reason. All of us who were baptised into Christ have put on Christ. "There is neither Jew nor Greek, there is neither bond nor free, there is neither male nor female for you are all one in Christ." (Galatians: 3.26) There is a trenchant reinforcement of this teaching in Chapter Four of the same epistle, where Paul states that because we are sons, God sent the Spirit of his Son into our hearts, crying, Abba, Father. Obviously, women do not receive a different spirit from God at conversion from that of men. They too can cry, "Abba, Father!" Everyone that is in Christ is a new creation. Old things have passed away. Everything is new. Therefore, all cultural differences that applied, apply, and will apply, relate only to Adam's race, and have no place in the true Church comprised of a new creation.

The concept of the family of God

Impartiality is an aspect of God's nature: He is not a respecter of persons. In other words he does not differentiate between men and women, and that is why He saves all those who repent while they are still sinners and admits them into His family by adoption. In the same way God found it unnecessary to amplify His teaching about 'Sons', Jesus also gave no preliminary teaching about the 'Father'. He began to speak about His Father easily and as a matter of course as an established fact. He associated all his followers with membership of the divine family and, therefore, as children of God. That is why Paul could write so confidently about the subject to the Church of the Galatians. Since the true Church is synonymous with the family of God, it follows that those of His family whom God sets in the Church as ministers need not be drawn exclusively from men.

A precedent

There is a heart-warming account of a husband and wife ministry in Acts Chapter 18. When Paul went to Corinth he met Aquila and Priscilla and worked with them. They were all tentmakers. It seemed they worshipped together every Sabbath when Paul preached in the synagogue. When Paul left Corinth for Ephesus their fellowship was so close that Aquila and Priscilla went with him. When Paul continued his missionary journey as promised husband and wife stayed behind and, obviously, became a teaching ministry team at Corinth. Then a Jew named Apollos came to Corinth. He was a highly educated man with a knowledge of the scriptures (that would be of the Old Testament) and spoke with great fervour. However, when Aquila and Priscilla heard him speak in the synagogue they quietly invited him to their home to explain the way of God more thoroughly. Until then Apollos understood only the baptism of John. So thoroughly did they teach him that Apollos went to Achaia and strengthened the Church in that place. He refuted the Jews in public, proving from the scriptures that Jesus was the Christ. Here we have a clear case of a woman teaching a man with the approval of the Church.

Witness from without

In Paul's estimate one of the desired qualities for leadership in the Church was for a member to have a good report from without. What better example can there be than that set by women missionaries in Nigeria between the years 1840 to 1960. When Nigeria gained its independence in 1960 it published a special independence issue of its national magazine. A majority of its population, based mainly in the north, followed the

Islamic faith whereas there were large numbers of Christians in the east and west as a result of missionary activities going back as far as 1840. The Muslims dominated the federal as well as the northern government but had no qualms in paying tribute to the contribution of Christian missionaries in bringing people out of darkness and laying the foundations of education and culture.

> "The first missionaries had no drugs and prophylactics and most of them died within a few months or years. West Africa was known as the white man's grave. They lived nearer to people than traders or officials, sharing their hardships, entering into their homes, learning their language, and sharing their burdens. Nobody is perfect but it was officially acknowledged that to the very limit of their resources they fed the hungry, cured the sick, freed the prisoner, sought mercy for the condemned and comforted those in sorrow. Their reward was seen to be simply in doing of it and nothing else. A dedicated missionary, Henry Townsend, who served in Abeokuta, wrote in his journal: 'This day renewed the vows I made to God two years since, to devote myself to His service in the missionary work with fresh entreaties for grace to enable me to go forth, with a single eye to His glory, and for full purpose of heart, not to return unless necessity compels me to do so, but to spend and be spent in His service, not seeking to please man but God.'
>
> "Another very heroic missionary was a woman, Mary Slessor, who worked chiefly among the up river tribes of Calabar province for 38 years. She sought to correct the notions of E K P E and witchcraft, to improve the status of women and children, to dispel fear and fight diseases. It is said that if you educate a man you educate an individual; if you educate a women you educate a family. Women could enter into an intimacy of understanding with the mothers of Nigeria which would be most improper and unbecoming in a man. There were other women at that time: 'Mammy' Sutherland of Calabar, Anna Hinderer of Ibadan, and Sara Townsend of Abeokuta."

In India there was the extraordinary Amy Carmichael of Donavar, and later Gladys Aylward in China whose exploits are recorded in *The*

Inn of the Sixth Happiness. Later Isobel Kuhn was equally fruitful and wrote brilliantly of her service in a series of bestselling books. These recorded God's wonderful works amongst the Lisu tribes. Returning from the missionary field with terminal cancer, she was spared for five years during which she had a prodigious literary output.

Of course, all these women shone primarily not because they were women but because they had become new creatures in Christ. They demonstrated that women could be effective in God's ministry. Their lives earned respect of people of other races and faiths.

Where God stands

An outstanding account of God's impartiality is apparent from the events of Pentecost recorded in the Acts of the Apostles. One hundred and twenty believers were present when the Holy Spirit fell on this assembly. thirteen men were named. That is the eleven remaining Apostles and the two who were to be subject to lots to replace the deceased Judas Iscariot. Mary the mother of Jesus was named. The remaining 106 persons consisted of the brothers of Jesus, the women and a number of other men. They were all filled with the Holy Spirit and were empowered to declare the wondrous works of God in such a way that the populace, representing various nations and tongues, understood what was being said. They were Galileans and the populace were Parthians, Medes, Elamites, residents of Mesopolitania, Judea and Cappodocia, Pontus and Asia, Phrygia and Pamphylia, Egypt and parts of Libya near Cyrenia; visitors from Rome (both Jews and converts to Judaism), Cretans, and Arabs.

The hearers were amazed and perplexed and after Peter explained the phenomenon and preached the gospel 3,000 people were added to the Church. God bestowed his power upon both men and women without differentiation because they were one in Christ having received the same spirit. Before moving into the following chapter in which the inclusion of other women in the work of God will be traced in other scriptures a marker needs to be put up.

To experience the power of the Holy Spirit was no less than receiving the promise of the Father. Paul said this was for all the followers, and their children, and as many as the Lord their God would call. Here again is the concept of an inclusive family and, prospectively, future families, once adopted, going on to receive the promise of the Father. In Paul's letter to the Galatians he makes it clear that any other teaching amounts to a gospel that is not a gospel at all!

Provisos

It is difficult to get one's head around the fact of impartiality. That is why, and only why, it is necessary to consider the matter of equality at all. When the subject of equality is broached visions of a worldly glass ceiling can be conjured up. "Glass ceiling" is a phrase used in the business and professional world to describe what is seen to be a level that only the most able women can get above. It has resulted in the introduction of artificial quotas by emancipators to promote more women, not necessarily on merit, in order to engineer more equal numbers of men and women executives. In God's kingdom such methods can never apply because these have no bearing at all on impartiality. Calling and gifting can have nothing to do with equal numbers. So it is much more helpful, in what is a topical debate, to bear continually in mind that it is the question of God's impartiality that I am majoring upon. It is vital, however, to allow the subject of equality to come to the fore as long as women are being blatantly disenfranchised. Hypothetically, there could at times be a preponderance of women overseers.

Impartiality and balance

As an illustration of a difference between equality and impartiality, take the case of Deborah who was a prophetess and a judge of Israel. She was both a theocratic leader and the possessor of a spiritual gift. Just read the fourth chapter of The Book of Judges. The fact that she was a woman shows us, clearly, that God is impartial. He was content with the appointment of a woman. The position, as far as we can tell, was that Deborah remained the only woman judge during the time of the Amphictyony. There was, therefore, a stark imbalance in sex representation. This does not spoil my case because God is not concerned with equality as such but with our obedience to his divine calling. God will call whosoever is the most spiritually equipped. This is underpinned in the Bible: and how helpful, thorough and constructive it is! He will not call reprobates. We encounter in the second and third chapters of Genesis two examples of the outworking of fallen nature. The man claims to be head of the woman and the woman is capable of being beguiled by the serpent. Claims of male supremacy have become a creed for macho organisations and allegations of feminine weaknesses a prop for those who argue for continued male dominance in the Church. Mercifully, the fourth chapter of Genesis heralds, prospectively, eventual newness of life and the introduction of glorious impartiality. A woman, the Virgin Mary, by the seed of the Holy Spirit, would become a vessel ushering in the incarnation of The Son of God, and He would crush the serpent's head. People will know the truth and the truth will set them free. That is freedom from the bondage of the dead letter through Christ Our Lord. Neither following tradition nor not following it avails anything…but a new creature. And, thanks be to God, gender will become irrelevant in the future earthly Kingdom of God, if not before!

Chapter Two

WOMEN IN THE OLD TESTAMENT

> "There are different kinds of service, but the same Lord. There are different kinds of working but the same God works all of them in all people." 1 Corinthians 2:4

The service of women

In God's estimate his people engage in wider forms of service for him than is generally recognised on earth. Therefore, more of us are involved in his service than we suppose. This fact is clear from my choice of servants in the following list. As far as women are concerned, God has always worked in them, but also the inclusion of some of them in His service is less obvious to us than are the exploits of others. Thus, Mary the mother of Jesus has a much higher profile than others that I am about to mention.

Eve

I hesitated before including Eve in this list and then concluded that we are inclined to be too hard on her; harder than the Lord God was. She was beguiled by the serpent and persuaded Adam to believe in the same lie. Yet the name Eve means life-giving. I confess that until recently I had a negative view of this woman. Having nursed a dear wife for four years I was deprived of the benefits of corporate fellowship. It was a time for reflection and contentment in whatever situation that arose. Then it came to saying, "the Lord gives, and the Lord takes away. Blessed be the name of the Lord". Renewed fellowship in a compassionate church brought me back into the once familiar atmosphere where we imperfect ones try to look through God's eyes on the struggling and the lost in this vale of tears. I am looking at Eve in such a context and avoiding elevated language. When Eve believed Satan rather than God who had provided the delights of Eden for her He must have been devastated. His holiness and righteousness obliged him to stick to His word. Death must result from disobedience. I had left the merciful and compassionate character of God out of this particular equation. He loves the world infinitely! I can imagine God thinking, "what a catastrophe! I cannot undo the immediate punishment but I can redeem this couple in the long run. I will begin by reassuring them and I will use a woman in a front running role in achieving a rescue. Satan beguiled a woman so another woman will bear one who will crush his head. Satan, through Adam brought in death. I will bring about the death of death through a second Adam. I will tell the serpent and tell the woman this so that she has a hope that is certain and true. Although she was disobedient in one respect I know she will be obedient in another. The world will not pay much attention to this but I will both remember and forgive. It will be recorded for posterity that I commanded Adam and Eve to increase and multiply and fill the earth (Genesis 1.28) and this they will do. I will in the fullness of time send my son born of a woman in order that...they might receive adoption...and I can send his spirit into their hearts." (Galatians: 4: 4, 5, 6).

The Virgin Mary

Mary was mentioned, firstly, in the Book of Genesis. She is not only blessed amongst women but also in the nations. All generations have called her "blessed". This handmaid of the Lord will be accorded a separate chapter because she was the second woman referred to above. I will pass on to deal below, firstly, with accounts of two women who are both lesser known for their role in God's purposes and who had lesser known spiritual gifts. Hopefully, these accounts will widen our appreciation of women who serve God in their generation.

Asenath

Asenath was Joseph's (the son of Jacob's) wife. She is mentioned in Genesis 41:45. She was the daughter of Potiphera, the priest of On, and was given to Joseph by Pharoah. She travelled with Joseph throughout Egypt. As well as supporting him in his work of saving the peoples of the Middle East and North West Africa from starvation she bore him two sons; Mannasseh and Ephraim. She was, therefore, the matriarch of two separate tribes of Israel. (Joshua 14:4) Joseph said of the first birth, "it is because God has made me forget all my trouble and all my father's household". Of the second birth he said, "it is because God has made me fruitful in the land of my suffering". It is all too easy to overlook Asenath when reading about Joseph, that spiritual giant who could interpret dreams. Although Joseph, rightfully, gave thanks to God, it is plain to me that Asenath was a divine instrument, bringing comfort and consolation to her husband in his trials. Her love was a compensation for his separation from kindred in a strange land. It also aided his success in the midst of suffering.

Zipporah

We can read in Exodus 2:21 that Moses had to flee from Egypt because he killed a man. He fled to Midian in the backside of the desert. After having spent all his childhood, youth, and early manhood as the adopted son of Pharaoh's daughter it must have been a terrible comedown. The luxury, privilege, and affluence of court was suddenly denied him. When Zipporah became his wife in Midian his circumstances were such that he sorely needed the love and support of a loyal partner. It has been said that Moses spent many years being somebody in Egypt and then many years being a nobody in Midian. The latter experience was a period of pruning and chastisement whereby God was able to make Moses a usable instrument. That is how our heavenly Father hones our lives today. And God gave Moses a wonderful helpmeet in Zipporah. As instructed by God Moses set out for Egypt with Zipporah and their sons. At a lodging place on the way Moses was struck down with a potentially fatal illness that we are told was inflicted by God (Exodus 4:24). Zipporah was sufficiently attuned to realise that the cause of God's anger was Moses' neglect to follow the Jewish custom with eight-day-old boys. Despite her repugnance she immediately rectified the omission and God relented. Although the passage is obscure, it is amplified in the Jewish Targum Onk and in the Hebrew there can be no other meaning. Jethro joined Moses and his family in the desert. He taught Moses the art of delegation which proved so valuable to him later. He then returned to Midian. It is reasonable to suppose that Zipporah remained with Moses and her sons and was part of their subsequent journeying. This stalwart wife in saving her husband's life ensured that Israel had an exemplary leader who would take God's people out of Egypt, establish the law, sojourn in the wilderness, effect the Red Sea crossing, and come to the brink of the promised land. God would have been hard put to find a replacement who could achieve his delivering purpose with quite the same effect.

Miriam

Miriam was the elder sister of Moses and Aaron. She watched over Moses, sang at the Red Sea and was smitten by leprosy when she murmured against Moses. She was called a prophetess, evidently, as appears from Numbers 12.2, because she had received divine communications. The word is used here in its proper sense of uttering words suggested by the Spirit of God. The part assigned to Miriam in the singing was in accordance with Hebrew and Egyptian customs. The men are represented as singing the hymn in chorus, under the guidance of Moses; at each interval Miriam and the women sang the refrain, marking the time with the timbrel, and with the measured rhythmical movements always associated with solemn festivities. Miriam sang, *Sing you to the Lord, for he has triumphed gloriously; the horse and his rider has He thrown into the sea!*

Rahab

In the second chapter of The Book of Joshua we are told how two spies were sent to look over the land of Canaan. They hid in the house of a prostitute named Rahab. The King of Jericho found out and expected Rahab to betray them. Instead of doing this she pretended they had already left; invited the king to go after them, and then hid them on her roof. She let them down by a rope through a window that was over the city wall, giving them instructions to hide in the hills for three days. Because of her bravery and kindness she was told to put a scarlet cord in her window when the Israelites invaded. This would ensure her safety. We might regard Rahab as being of dubious repute, but God used her. In his annals she is forever remembered. In Hebrews, Chapter 12 there is a list of God's champions of outstanding faith like Abraham, Isaac, Jacob, Joseph and Moses. And there the Holy-Spirit-inspired verse (31) includes Rahab, "by faith the prostitute Rahab, because she welcomed the spies, was not killed with those who were disobedient". She is also mentioned in the letter of James (2.25, 26). "Was not Rahab the Harlot also justified by works, when she received the messengers and sent them out another way? For just as the body without the spirit is dead, so also faith without works is dead!"

Ruth

A woman of exemplary character, Ruth is accorded her own book in the Bible. She ensured the continuity of the line of David by giving birth to Obed who was David's grandfather.

Hannah

In the first book of Samuel we read that Hannah was the mother of this great prophet. She was also a prophetess, as is proved by the prophecy contained in her hymn of thanksgiving for the birth of her son. It is in the highest order of prophetic poetry. It contains the first designation of the *Messiah under that name (BC 1121). "My heart exults in the Lord, My horn is exalted in the Lord, My mouth speaks boldly against my enemies, Because I rejoice in Thy salvation, There is no one holy like the Lord, Indeed there is no one besides Thee, Nor is there any rock like our God..."*

The Queen of Sheba

This queen had heard about Solomon's God in her own land and was anxious to learn more. Having visited Solomon she said that she had not believed these things until she came and saw with her own eyes. Not even half had been told to her. Because, she said, of the Lord's love for Israel, he has made him King to maintain justice and righteousness. On return to her country she would have spread the faith. Sheba was a land in Africa near the Straits of Babel-mandeb. It is probable that the growth of Jewish believers in Ethiopia was due to the influence of this queen. In Acts 51 we can read of the Ethiopian eunuch, an official in the court of Queen Candice. He was in possession of the Book of Isaiah the Prophet!

Esther

This Jewish woman married King Xerxes and was instrumental in saving her nation from Haman's evil plot to destroy it. She showed great courage in daring to speak out to the king in defence of Mordecai. The tables were turned and the hanging Haman had planned for Mordecai was, instead, inflicted upon him.

Dispensations

Those mentioned so far, lived during the times of the Old Testament. None had received what had been promised. Some only knew of the promise to Abraham and some lived under the law with, as it were, a veil over their face. Those mentioned in the next chapter knew of the mystery hidden from the ages which is Christ in us, the hope of glory, and lived in the present dispensation of the receipt of His spirit: a period when God's impartiality was more fully revealed. We can reflect, before passing on, upon the way God used the women listed above despite the fact that they belonged to past dispensations who were not fully aware of the future glorious liberty of those who would become God's children. However, such liberty would remain largely a potential in God's permissive will and, disappointingly, be elusive in reality.

The recent beginnings of wider recognition of women in the Church can be taken as a countersign. The enemy is coming in like a flood so we must look to the spirit of the Lord to raise up a standard. In pulling down the strongholds of professing religion there will follow an exposure of the fallacies contained in the traditions of men. Women will, increasingly, play their rightful part in the expansion of God's kingdom. It will be recognised that we already have many of them in the Church who are ready and that this includes those with less recognisable spiritual gifts that should not be overlooked. For instance there are those able to help others, and those with the gifts of administration (1 Corinthians 12:28).

Fate of women

I cannot pass on to the New Testament before expressing my views about two very sad incidents in which women suffered misfortune. The first was an accident and I need do no more than show that men did their best and that God gave very fair warning. Lot's wife was turned into a pillar of salt when she looked back at Sodom and Gomorrah. God had warned Abraham's party of the dangers of looking back. (Genesis: 19) He had also told Lot to flee up the mountain. Lot was unwilling to do this and obtained permission to flee to Zoar, a little place nearby. This obviously made things more hazardous. Pieces of glass recovered from this area by archaeologists showed signs of having been subjected to greater heat than that generated by atom bombs.

The case of Jephthah's daughter is a horrifying one, and it bears out my case against certain elements of male thinking. It is recorded in Judges 11 that Jephthah wanted to avenge himself against the children of Ammon and vowed that if his desires were granted he would make a burnt offering of the first thing he set his eyes upon afterwards. Unfortunately, this turned out to be his daughter. Expositors have struggled with this account; giving all kinds of dubious explanations of possibilities of a reprieve. One cannot get away from the stark facts. A vow was made and the vow was kept. This was a most appalling crime and the writer of Judges had the insensitivity to record the facts in a completely neutral manner.

His style was as if God approved both the vow and the bestial consequence! We are not supposed to vow but to let our no be no and our yes be yes! There is no condemnation in Judges of this act. It is almost as though the writer was accepting the action as inevitable. God spared Isaac, so, clearly, God does not approve of human sacrifice. In fact God strictly forbade the practice of making children pass through the fire. In II Kings, the kings of Israel were condemned for the evil practice of making their sons and daughters pass through the fire. This incident brings home to us the dangers of imagining one is in the will of God when in reality one is encountering false creations of the mind.

Chapter Three

WOMEN IN THE NEW TESTAMENT

> And Mary said, "Behold the handmaid of the Lord; be it done unto me according to your word." Luke 1.35

Living in the Lord's Day

If I found my task of reviewing lives of faithful women in the Old Testament very uplifting, how much more will those I have chosen to include here stir me beyond measure. These women lived in the days of Jesus' earthly ministry. They walked, talked and dined with him. They were blessed by his gracious words, they were amazed at his miracles, grieved at his rejection, and wept when he suffered and died. Some were at the cross, and some saw him after his ascension and after his resurrection. I highlight here how these also supported him financially and ministered to his needs as he went through cities and villages. I will boldly assert that these women had a greater propensity for manifesting pity and unconditional love than did the men who were their contemporaries.

A proverbial argument

Today some men argue that, biblically, women should be barred from serving God in prime roles. For instance they introduce circumstantial evidence. Jesus, they say, only chose men as apostles. I am going to show in this chapter that women are not second-class Christians in the eyes of the Holy Spirit. In fact the call of some of them in the past was more endearing than the call of some men.

Jesus called his first four apostles as he was walking by the Sea of Galilee. Seeing these fishermen, he called them to follow Him. He would make them fishers of men. They immediately left their nets and followed Him.

Now, God's approach to the Virgin Mary was more commendatory. The Archangel Gabriel announced that she had found favour with God and her response was one of total readiness. It is printed at the top of this chapter.

Elizabeth

Elizabeth was the wife of Zacharias and the mother of John the Baptist. She was a relative of Mary the mother of Jesus. What a unique moment of exhilaration and joy was experienced by these favoured women when they met. Their Holy Spirit-inspired utterances have been recorded so that we can draw inspiration from them. I feel sure you will be as abundantly blessed when reading these as I have been in writing them. First of all, let me remind you of the background.

The angel, when announcing Mary's impending conception, also told her that Elizabeth was already six months pregnant in her old age. Mary went at once to the house of Zacharias and met Elizabeth. Then this great Holy Spirit encounter took place. The baby leaped in Elizabeth's womb, and Elizabeth was filled with the Holy Spirit. She exercised the spiritual gift of knowledge. In a loud voice she said to Mary, *Blessed among women are you, and blessed is the fruit of your womb. And how has it happened to me that the mother of my Lord should come to me? And blessed is she who believed that there would be a fulfilment of what had been spoken to her by her Lord.*

Mary ecstatically uttered the most sublime of prayers. Here was prophecy, edification and rejoicing! *My soul exalts the Lord, and my spirit rejoices in God my Saviour, for he had regard for the humble state of His handmaid; for behold from this time on all generations will call me blessed. For the Mighty One has done great things for me; and holy is His name. And His mercy is upon generation after generation towards those who fear Him. He has done mighty deeds with His arm; He has scattered those who were proud in the thoughts of their heart. He has brought down rulers from their thrones, and He has exalted those who were humble. He has filled the hungry with good things; and sent away the rich empty handed.*

Mary stayed for about three months and soon after this Elizabeth gave birth to John the Baptist of whom it was prophesied by Zacharias that he would be called the Prophet of the Most High, for he would go before the Lord to prepare His ways to give his people the knowledge of salvation by the forgiveness of their sins. This also confirmed a prophecy given by Malachi many generations previously (see Malachi 3.1).

What a mountain-top experience was afforded these two women of God and what a shame when we have to descend to the valley to consider more mundane aspects of the role of women.

Anna

We don't have to go down the mountain just yet. When I reflect upon the lives of Anna and her companion of the temple, Simeon, I want to go higher up the mountain. I feel like singing the old hymn, *Lead me higher up the mountain into fellowship with Thee, in the light I see the fountain and the blood that ransomed me. Jesus bring me higher up the mountain where the spirit comes in flood...*

Anna was a prophetess, the daughter of Phanuel, of the tribe of Aser: she was elderly. She had lived with her husband for seven years, and had been a widow for eighty-four years. During the whole of her widowhood she had remained in the temple, serving God with fastings and prayers night and day. What an encouragement this woman is to all whose partner has left this world first. It can be taken for granted that she had been a great help to her husband and that they had served the Lord together. Once she was on her own she found great satisfaction in being, not alone, but in communion with God. Likewise every Christian need never feel alone. Yes, one might retire into an otherwise empty house. It does not feel empty because God is present by his spirit. (*I will never be alone, because Father God you are there beside me.)*

I don't know whether Anna's expectations of seeing her Messiah stemmed from personal revelation or whether she learned from Simeon. I like to think that on account of her steadfastness, the Holy Spirit showed the future to both and gave both of them the same promise. The Bible is not explicit but whether these revelations were independent or shared they were obviously both party to their content.

It does mean that I have to rely upon Simeon's account to follow what preceded the meeting with Jesus in the temple as recorded in Luke's gospel (2.27). The Holy Spirit had revealed to him that he would not die until he had seen the promised Messiah. He came by the spirit into the temple and you can read that he took Jesus in his arms and uttered an extraordinary prophecy. I will refer to this in the following chapter.

Of course, Anna was already in the temple. She gave thanks to the Lord as Simeon had already done and spoke of him to all that looked for the redemption of Israel. They were both inspired by the Holy Spirit and had identified promises in earlier prophetic words of the coming of the Messiah with the coming of Jesus into the temple. They were directly inspired to know they would not see death before they had seen the Lord's Christ.

They also would have known of God's word and that the word and the spirit are always in agreement (1 John 5.8). Returning to Malachi's remarkable prophecy: this stated, "*And the Lord whom you seek shall come suddenly to his temple: even the messenger of the covenant whom you delight in: Behold he shall come saith the Lord of Hosts*" (3:1). He came to his temple as a babe in arms. They would also have known of Jacob's foreknowledge as recorded in Genesis 49:10, "*The sceptre shall not depart from Judah, nor a law giver from between his feet until Shiloh come and unto to him shall the gathering of the people be.*" The promise of Jacob to Judah (Jesus' tribe) was fulfilled. Its authority continued until the destruction of Jerusalem in AD 70. Judah never ceased to be a tribe until Shiloh came. (Shiloh is the Hebrew name for the Messiah as Prince of Peace, or as the "seed" of Judah.) When the temple was destroyed many people in Jewry realised that there was no longer a possibility of another person being able to make a convincing claim to be the Messiah.

The Marys

Seven women by the name of Mary were privileged to be followers of Jesus and a degree of concentration is necessary in order to distinguish between them. For instance, what is not readily apparent is that there were two occasions when women anointed Jesus. One of these women was Mary, the sister of Lazarus and Martha and the other was Mary Magdalene. I am going to list all the Marys here for your information:

1. The mother of Jesus and wife of Joseph.
2. Mary Magdalene.
3. Mary the mother of James the less, Joses and Salome.
4. Mary the wife of Cleophas.
5. Mary the sister of Lazarus and Martha.

6. Mary the mother of John Mark.
7. Mary a female believer in Rome who helped Paul.

Mary Magdalene

When Jesus was invited by Simon, the Pharisee, to dinner Mary brought an alabaster box of ointment, stood at His feet and began to wash them with tears and wipe them with her hair. She then kissed His feet and anointed them with the ointment. The Pharisees were scandalised, saying that if Jesus was a prophet He should have known what manner of woman this was: for she was a sinner. But Jesus said, her sins were forgiven; for she loved much: but to whom little is forgiven the same loves little. Jesus had previously cast out seven devils from her. Mary became one of a contingent of women who accompanied Him through cities and villages. I will not be mentioning the other women elsewhere so it is good to list them. They were Joanna the wife of Chuza Herod's steward, and Susanna and many others. They all ministered to Jesus and supported Him financially. The attitude of the disciples was somewhat different. They wanted to bring down fire on the Samaritans, connived to extract a promise about being able to sit next to Jesus in the eternal Kingdom, and tried to prevent children from getting His blessing.

We read of this Mary again at the cross. The events at the cross, at the tomb, and at the resurrection need to be pieced together from the records of Matthew, Mark, Luke and John. Mary Magdalene was at the cross and stayed on when Joseph of Aramathea took Jesus down and had Him laid in his own tomb. She sat outside the sepulchre for some time. The next day before it was light she went back. Other women came later with sweet spices to anoint the body. Seeing the stone that had sealed the tomb was rolled away, they went in. Inside were two angels and one of them told them not to be afraid. Jesus was not there; He had risen. They must tell his disciples and Peter. They ran away, frightened and amazed, and told nobody.

Mary lingered and Jesus appeared to her. She was, therefore, the first person to meet the risen Lord and also with the other Mary to tell Peter and the disciples. They did not believe her. However Peter and John went to the empty tomb but since they did not understand the doctrine of the resurrection at this time they went home. Mary's encounter was tender. She thought she had met the gardener. Then she heard, "Mary" and replied "Rabboni" – My Rabbi (Aramaic). It is obvious that Mary was privileged and that she showed a steadfastness that was lacking in others. It can be safely assumed that Mary was present at Pentecost, and, a member of the early Church.

Mary the mother of James the Less

This Mary figured quite prominently in the events surrounding the passion, death and resurrection of Jesus. She stood afar off at the cross. She sat with Mary Magdalene outside the sepulchre and then she went back with her early the following morning. She went into the empty tomb with her, heard the angel's instructions and was terrified.

Mary Cleophas

Mary Cleophas mourned at the cross. Here was a woman who was not afraid of the Jewish authorities and the hostile crowds. With the exception of John the male followers of Jesus had run away.

Mary the sister of Lazarus and Martha, at Bethany

It was to this household that Jesus came to relax from His arduous itineraries. The companionship meant a great deal to Jesus and it is hard to imagine what it was like to this family to entertain the Son of God. They, poor things, were only human. The sisters bickered about Mary's choice of sitting at Jesus' feet and listening to His word and Martha's lot serving and washing up. Jesus was, no doubt, bemused at the realistic domestic atmosphere. He thought Mary had chosen the good part and deserved it.

I am grateful that John preserved for us the account of the raising of Lazarus from the dead. He tells us that Jesus loved this family. When Jesus was in another place Lazarus fell ill and Mary and Martha went and told him. Having said the sickness was not to death but for God's glory, Jesus stayed for three days in the same place. After this he decided to go back to Bethany even though Thomas tried to dissuade Him on the grounds of danger. Jesus had insight that Lazarus was dead and said so. By the time Jesus arrived in the vicinity Lazarus had been in the grave for four days. Martha is shown in a favourable light when she went out to meet Jesus and this is what we should remember about her. After saying that if Jesus had been there earlier her brother need not have died she went further by saying, "but I know, that even now, whatsoever you will ask of God, God will give it to you". She also believed in the resurrection of the dead at the last day – something the Sadducees denied! Then came a wonderful confession of her belief in Jesus as the Christ, the Son of God. She then went and told Mary that Jesus was nearby.

Jesus entered Bethany and went to the graveside and wept. On calling Lazarus forth, all who stood there saw he who was dead come forth bound up in grave clothes. He was loosed and reunited with his sisters. There are several things we should note:

1. Words cannot fully capture the moment when Lazarus came forth from the grave at the command of Jesus or describe adequately the ecstasy and heartfelt gratitude of Mary and Martha.

2. It is recorded that Jesus once raised a ruler's daughter from the dead. He raised the son of the widow of Nain, and Lazarus the brother of Mary and Martha. Could it be that Jesus was exceptionally moved by the deep sorrows of the women? I will return to this possibility when writing about His mother.

3. Jesus risked being stoned when entering Judea and it turned out that in raising the dead He undermined the authority of the Sanhedrin. Their spies were present and reported the incident at once. They could not raise the dead so this Galilean had to be got rid of.

4. As great as this act was, Lazarus died eventually and so did the widow's son, and the ruler's daughter. Elijah was taken up to heaven alive, and he will come back to die. Jesus is the only one to have died and come back to life permanently in the body. He exclaimed triumphantly, "I am He that liveth, and was dead; and, behold, I am alive for evermore Amen; and have the keys of hell and of death!

Mary Mark

She was the mother of Mark, the writer of the second synoptic gospel, and thought to be the secretary to Peter. All we know about her is that she was one of a band of believers during a period of severe persecution by Herod. When Peter was released supernaturally from prison by an angel the believers would not at first believe it was him; then they were astonished. Peter had to go to another place for his own safety. It is not surprising that the indigenous faithful had to face the venom of Herod's wrath. However, God was on their side. First of all they made friends with Herod's chamberlain, and then Herod made a speech that glorified himself. He was smitten by an angel (maybe the one who freed Peter from prison?), and he died. But the word of God grew and multiplied. What an accomplishment of John Mark and his mother! He left and went to Antioch with Paul and Barnabus. He fell out of the work at one stage. After all he was very young. Later he was greatly used when working with Peter.

Dorcas

Dorcas (also known as Tabitha) was a follower of Peter at Joppa. She was known for her good works and alms deeds. One day she fell sick and died. Peter was summoned and when he went to her bedroom all the widows were weeping and showing him the coats and garments which Dorcas made (these were probably intended for the needy). Peter prayed and said, Tabitha arise. She sat up and was presented to the widows alive.

Lydia

Lydia was a seller of purple in Philippi. Each Sabbath a number of women there met by the river to pray. These were led by Lydia, a native of Thyatira, who worshipped God. Paul came to preach at the river and Lydia heard him and her heart was opened. After being baptised, she asked Paul to judge whether she was being faithful to the Lord, and if she passed the test, suggested he might come to her house to live. Paul and Timothy were glad to join her and no doubt her abode became a centre of witness.

It is interesting that the risen Lord commanded the apostle John to write a letter to the Church at Thyatira. This commended it for good works, love, service and faith. It appears that the legacy of Lydia remained with them. But there was also a false and immoral prophetess who seduced them. There were many who were not deceived but they were guilty of failing to oppose sufficiently all that was dishonouring. In a later chapter I will be writing about false prophets who operate at the present time. I will include women but make it clear that it is unfair to cite their behaviour as an excuse to denigrate women per se. Just as God is impartial as to whom He chooses so the ordinary laws of chance and probability turn up both false men and false women.

Lois

Lois was Timothy's grandmother. He had been inspired and taught by Lois and his mother Eunice from childhood. Here was a clear case of a man being taught by women. It is thought that at the time Paul told Timothy not to let people despise his youth he would have been forty-seven years of age.

The Syrophenician woman

It appears that this Greek national was a pagan. Her daughter had an unclean spirit and, hearing of Jesus' growing reputation for deliverances, came and fell at His feet. He rebuffed her. Seeing that Jesus had foreknowledge it is obvious that He was putting her to the test. He said that anyone who came to Him He would in no wise cast out. It is written that in one place He healed them all. Having been told it was not right to cast the children's bread to the dogs, she countered by pointing out that dogs under the table eat the children's crumbs. That was sufficient. Because of her response to Jesus her daughter was delivered. On reaching her house this woman found that the devil had gone out.

The diseased woman

A woman who had suffered from a serious blood disorder for twelve years came up behind Jesus in the throng and touched the hem of His garment. Being aware that virtue had gone out of Him Jesus asked who had caused this and His followers denied it was any of them; whereupon the women fell, trembling at His feet and owned up. She had been healed instantaneously. Her faith had made her whole.

The Samaritan woman

When Jesus met this woman at the well He was not only prepared to speak to one who was a woman on her own; who was a Samaritan, and who was an adulteress. He entrusted her with the words of life knowing that she would receive these without reservation and go and tell others in the village who would also believe. So great was her conviction that many others went out to meet Jesus to hear Him for themselves. They besought Him to stay, which He did for two days, and many of them believed in Him.

The listed special or normative?

The long list of women I have portrayed so far, who have been used or favoured by God, constitutes a powerful case, itself in support of my contention about divine impartiality. God did not distinguish against any of these women but used them all at his own discretion.

In the next chapter I have written more fully about the Virgin Mary. It was important that I devoted more space to this most key person of all women. After this I enter the lists against those who I know will argue, despite my evidence so far, that women still do not have a universal right to impartial access to God's job vacancies.

Chapter Four

MARY THE MOTHER OF JESUS

> "The angel said, Hail thou that are highly favoured, the Lord is with thee: blessed art thou amongst women." Luke 1:28.

Early years

This Mary is, undoubtedly, the most favoured of all people ever born of mankind. As the handmaid of the Lord she stands out as an example of obedience, faithfulness, and how to suffer willingly. I have already written much about her because her life impacted upon so many others. She was destined from the outset to be a channel of God's grace in His great rescue plan for fallen humanity. She figured in the pronouncements of Old Testament prophets A virgin would conceive and bear a son whose name would be Immanuel – God with us. The deliverer would come out of the root of Jesse who figured in Mary's genealogy. So, she was amongst those who were heralded.

The angel had explained she would give birth to the Son of the Highest and that her conception would be supernatural. At this point Mary must have realised problems would arise. People would think her son was illegitimate. Nasty historians in our day gossip about an association with a Roman soldier. At the annunciation Mary did not know that God would ease her embarrassment by speaking to the one to whom she was betrothed. Initially, she was totally willing, come what may, unlike Gideon who was reticent or Moses who was reluctant.

God in His kindness prepared Mary for the sorrows she would face. He began, thoughtfully, by bringing the shepherds and wise men to Bethlehem and sending choirs of angels. He put the joyous side first.

Then he revealed through Simeon, firstly, the glory and then followed by warning of stark tragedy. And Mary kept these things in her heart. It was, indeed, a tough time when Herod's jealousy obliged the new family to flee into Egypt. They were refugees and times would have been hard for Mary with her infant. The journey outwards would have been arduous. One day Joseph learned through a dream that Herod was dead and he returned safely to Nazareth. However, since Herod's son Archelaus reigned in Judea he was afraid. The massacre of the innocents in Rama was hard to forget. That is why they resettled in Nazareth in Galilee. It is possible they knew of Isaiah's prophecy: He shall be called a Nazarene. They were granted thirty happy years of family life except for the scare when Jesus became separated in Jerusalem and was found debating with elders in the temple. It would be strange for Joseph to hear the lad say that he must be about His father's business. But it was not strange to Mary.

However, memories grow dim over time. Tradition has it that Jesus had a normal boyhood and learned the skills of carpentry from Joseph. It is supposed that at some stage Joseph died and Jesus would have become the breadwinner until the age of thirty. Although it is disputed by some that there were siblings, there is a contrary view that James was a brother in the close sense, and that there were two sisters who married. Mary would have been the mother of the household all those years. Mothers are special in Jewish culture.

The emergent son

When Jesus went to Jordan to be baptised by His cousin, John the Baptist, He was anointed by the Holy Spirit, and commenced His ministry. He must have caused an upheaval. The people must have wondered where He had gone after he was driven into the wilderness for forty days. Then when he returned and read from the scroll of Isaiah in the temple, and claimed that these scriptures spoke of him the people were outraged. Was He not Joseph the carpenter's son? The Messiah was to hail from Bethlehem? It was only Mary who knew the real facts. She would keep her head below the parapet. The tragedy of Rama was still with her. People were clambering for wonders such as followed Jesus' ministry in Capernaum. Not only was He impervious to their pressure; He stirred them up by saying that in the days of Elias when there was famine, He was only sent to one widow although there were many widows in Israel. Further, there were many lepers in the days if Eliseus but only Naaman the Syrian was healed. The people were so angry that they attempted, unsuccessfully, to throw Jesus over a cliff.

This worried His family no end. Not only this. His siblings did not, at that time, believe in Him. Clearly, Mary feared for His safety and also dreaded that their hitherto happy existence was ended forever. When the family came to remonstrate with Jesus His disciples told Him His mother and brothers were outside. He queried who His mother and brothers were. Looking about He said they were all those who did the will of God; the same were His mother and brother. In another account we are told that when a woman called from the crowd blessing Mary for nursing Him, He said that rather it was all who heard the word of God and kept it that should be blessed. Why did He say these things? After all He loved His mother to the extent of changing water and wine for her at Canaan. There are two possible answers. Firstly, He was driving home the fact that in Christ we are all one in a divine family. Secondly, the Holy Spirit preserved His remarks for posterity knowing that people would elevate humanity. They would ascribe to Mary certain attributes that belong only to God. By doing this they were not doing the word of God. In no way was Jesus putting His own family down. Rather, He was keeping its memory on a rational level. His words would come down through the ages as a counter to the wiles of those who would portray His family as being superhuman and thus mar the reality.

The virgin birth

Having stressed that Mary was a member of the human race, and a wonderful one, I will move on to higher ground: indeed, sacred ground. Mary was a channel in a momentous divine action. Among the greatest teachings in the Bible is the doctrine of the incarnation, otherwise called the virgin birth. Those who deny its truth are throwing the news of our salvation and God's ultimate victory out of the window. The cross of Christ was the culmination of our redemption. It could not have been accomplished, however, without a divine and sinless incarnation. We did not commit the sin of Adam and Eve: we inherited Adam's sinful nature because we are his progeny. But we cannot shrug off our personal culpability. Mary was not sinless, as some would have it. As Thomas Aquinas taught in his *Summa*, Mary rejoiced in Christ her Saviour. But that which was born of her was the spotless Son of God because He was not born of the will of man but by the power of the Holy Spirit. Let us look kindly on those who elevate Mary above her station. These are sincerely captivated and carried away by her virtue. Yet others tend, probably on account of the excessive adulation of virtuous human beings, to be disappointingly cold about her rightful blessedness. Liberals do not believe in the virgin birth and so miss its critical importance. The overriding joy is that Jesus was the first-born of a new creation. Let us praise Mary that He the first born was born of her! Jesus said that except a corn of wheat fall into the ground and die it abides alone. If it dies it brings forth much fruit. Jesus the fruit of Mary's womb died that He might bring many sons and daughters to glory. (Hebrews 2:10)

Her sorrow

Mary went through a sorrowful time when her beloved son was arrested, faced a mock trial and unjust condemnation. The brutality of His scourging, the crown of thorns, the carrying of the cross, and the horrors of a Roman crucifixion brought cruelly home to her, the prediction of Simeon that a sword would pierce her soul. As she stood at the cross it must have been like a ghastly nightmare to her and even John's support could not have been immediately appreciated. It has come to me that Mary is not mentioned as having been at the tomb with the other two Marys. Is it any wonder? She would have been overwhelmed and inconsolable in her grief and totally numb. She may not, along with Peter and John, have fully taken in the meaning of resurrection. She knew her son was the Messiah and the Saviour. How understandable it would be if she had not thought through the reality of an immediate rising again!

We know that Mary Magdalene and Joanna and Mary the mother of James (not James the Lord's brother) and other women went to the eleven apostles and told them about the empty tomb and the angels and they did not believe them. When Peter and John went to the empty tomb they did not realise its significance. No wonder two disciples on the Emmaus road were rebuked by the risen Lord, "O fools, and slow of heart to believe all the prophets have spoken." Later the Lord appeared in the upper room. There is no mention of His mother's presence and I will conjecture about a possible reason. It may have been that she was still grieving or it may have been that those gathered represented a male gathering. It is heart-warming to realise that she was present on the day of Pentecost (as I have already noted).

Having been brought up in orthodoxy I was attuned to understanding Mary's sorrows. It was customary and sobering to meditate on what was known as the Seven Dolours of Mary (Dolour-Latin: meaning grief, lamentation). I must confess it is only recently that I have thought about her longer-drawn-out anxieties. I have already mentioned her worry about Simeon's prophecy which she hid in her heart; and that it may have lain dormant throughout her happier years. Then there was the worry about the high profile of her son's ministry and its affect upon the authorities. His cousin lost his life for speaking out against Herod Antipas. Was Jesus heading for a showdown as well?

Mary lived through a series of events starting with the agony in Gethsemane and ending at the cross:

1. The agony in the garden.
2. The betrayal.
3. Taken to the high priest's room adjoining the booth of Hana.
4. Examination before Caiaphas and Sanhedrin at an irregular meeting.
5. Formal sentence of Sanhedrin in their proper place of meeting – Beth Midras.
6. The first examination before Pilate.
7. The examination before Herod Antipas.
8. The scourging and first mockery of the soldiers at the palace.
9. The sentence of Pilate.
10. The second mocking of the soldiers of the condemned "king".
11. The crucifixion and the rejection of the stupefying draught.
12. The last charge.
13. The darkness.
14. The end.

Mary may have found the silence of Jesus hard to endure. The exception must have proved both awesome and frightening for her. The high priest adjured Jesus by the living God to tell him whether He was the Son of God. The reply was that he would see the Son of Man sitting at the right hand of the seat of power and coming in the clouds of heaven. Poor Mary!

Anxiety

In order to bring home more fully the painfulness of psychological infliction of this kind I will give a contemporary example. It is becoming more common for British nationals to be taken hostage in other parts of the world. Sometimes these are murdered, sometimes they are released, and sometimes their fate is unknown. Ultimately there is grief, or rejoicing, or an indeterminable suspense. In every case there is a period of uncertainty and this is almost as painful to bear as is the moment when there is news of a fatality. Mary would have hoped that Jesus would be released by Pilate and not Barabbas.

Schism

The Christian Church has been racked with controversy over Mary's status in eternity. Orthodoxy imported a growing sense of mysticism. Tradition admitted beliefs in an immaculate conception, an assumption into heaven, a coronation as Queen of Heaven, an accolade as Star of the Sea. Mary is given a form of worship (dulia), is prayed to, can intercede, and was dubbed "mediatrix" in the documents of the Second Vatican Council of 1962. There has been Vatican verification of claims of earthly appearances and messages given. There are Marian altars in Orthodox and Anglican churches. Greek and Russian traditions attribute sacramental power to icons of Mary and this is beyond the Roman rite. Since the Reformation a substantial part of Christianity has disowned these traditions, regarding their origins as "extra-Biblical". One can be conciliatory without being concessionary. For example, by trying to understand why others adopt beliefs in the first place. One can deduce from scripture that Mary will have received exceptional reward in heaven on account of her exemplary earthly service and overcoming. This is not connected with her salvation. So Mariolatry can be allied to imaginative speculation. As such it need not be regarded as heinous. It does, in my opinion, distract many from admiration of the actual facts of her existence and also, of course, from the glory of her Son. Exactly how Mary is revered in heaven is hardly a subject for human deliberation.

Relevant to misogyny

I am primarily concerned about the role of Mary on earth as a woman. It may be questioned why I needed to bring in the controversy about her eternal sojourn. I have already partly answered by pointing out how heavenly notions can eclipse earthly realities. But there is a far more telling and challenging reason for choosing to raise this sensitive issue. It is too important a factor in my argument against hardened misogynists to be left out. The very men who took licence in promoting mystical Marian dogmas that magnified and venerated a woman, were also the very ones who were guilty of subjugating women by depriving them of their God-given right to be called without impartiality to serve in every aspect of the present kingdom. God has translated all believers into the kingdom of His dear Son. I am, therefore, justified in making this point but I hope that in doing so my strictures have not appeared to bc impolite.

Chapter Five

SILENCE OF THE WOMEN

"...Let the women keep silent in the Church." 1. Timothy 2:11

A scriptural argument

Depending upon your disposition there is a likelihood that you may cry, laugh, or disagree with the case I am making against the gagging of women. Those of the latter persuasion impede the path of liberty by resting on a single scripture and taking that scripture out of its context, whilst ignoring several other scriptures showing that women prayed audibly in the Church. I am confining my coverage to women in this chapter and will write elsewhere about some pastors' hesitance to allow anyone to pray spontaneously in services. Happily the selective silencing of women is no longer a common practice, but it is useful to know how the custom took root and what scriptural arguments were put forward to justify it.

A single scripture

It is dangerous to rely on a single scripture when seeking to introduce customs that are prohibitive. In fact the scripture shown above has nothing to do with praying at all. It cannot possibly have such a meaning because other scriptures record instances of women praying in church. The first epistle of Paul to the Corinthians contains teaching about conducting corporate worship. He writes about what to do when they come to pray together. For instance, if a woman prays or prophesies with her head uncovered it dishonours her head. I ask how could a woman so pray, and then at the same time stay silent. Philip had four daughters who prophesied and New Testament prophecy is for the purpose of edifying the Church. If these were obliged to prophesy under their breath, how could such behaviour possibly edify anybody? On the day of Pentecost a number of women spoke of the wonderful works of God and people from all over understood what they were saying in their own languages. How could these have heard anything if the women had to remain in mute mode?

Apostolic culture

Since scripture is consistent a wider reference to the meaning of "silence" serves to provide a fuller explanation. Why is this not done by those who oppose women? Another scripture helps my case. In the fourteenth chapter of the same Corinthian epistle women are again taught to be silent. "It is a shame for women to speak in the Church." But the context is helpful. "If they will learn anything, let them ask their husbands when they get home." In those times women sat together on one side of the Church and men sat on the other side. They were not to call out to ask their husbands if they did not understand the sermon. It was too disruptive. They must ask their husbands when they got home. Paul's injunction had nothing to do with praying.

A plague on chapels

This single scripture about silence has not bothered the orthodox one way or the other because women do not count in their estimation anyway. But it proved to be a plague on nonconformists. Orthodoxy has been regulated by an overriding priesthood and is most concerned about its exercise of authority over women in all matters. In chapels, meeting houses, and halls women were denied equal rights with men for hundreds of years. In some denominations women were not even allowed to pray audibly even at weekday prayer meetings. One chapel reached a state when only two men were left in fellowship and this meant they were obliged to pray in turns for an hour while twenty or so women sat silently.

I was an external trustee of a chapel for many years. Whenever I preached there I was impressed with the authentic behaviour and the solemn and precious moments in breaking-of-bread services. Men were free to stand up and bring their thoughts about scriptures, spontaneously, to the assembly. Unfortunately there was a hang-up over the single verse in 1: Timothy, about women keeping silent. The women were excluded. It eventually caused a dilemma. A bright, educated and eloquent young lady started to attend meetings. In all innocence, not knowing of the local shibboleth, she encroached upon the men's privileged domain with gusto. And she impressed everybody. Even the ranks of Tuscany could scarce forbear to cheer!

The gentle natured leaders did not have the heart to confront her. They turned to me for advice. Up to this point I had thought discretion was the better part of valour. I preached across denominational lines and was glad for freedom to explain the gospel without getting involved with idiosyncrasies. However, in this circumstance I was well and truly put on the spot. I had no option but to express my views as already set out here. To my surprise they listened and then acceded to my points.

At the next meeting of the trustees they seemed chastened, bruised, but distinctly unbowed. I was right but how could they possibly liberate younger women precipitately? There were mature women brought up in the movement from childhood who had never been able to pray audibly in public during the whole of their long lives. Two women who were notable pillars of the work were cited as an example of those who would be upset if a young lady, and a newcomer at that, was allowed to continue to hold forth. I did not know what to say.

It so happened that by custom when I preached twice on Sundays I had lunch with one leader and tea with another. It also happened that when I went to preach the next time that I was served lunch by the first named women and tea by the second. I tackled them about their reported misgivings. One said she had been born in China of missionary parents and on the mission field women had to be prepared to do anything including preaching and praying. She had no objection to the young women bringing their thoughts in public or to women praying in the chapel in services. The other woman had been a nurse. She expressed surprise that the men had attributed such views to her. She concurred with the first woman. So that was set and match as far as I was concerned. I needed to say nothing. The dilemma was solved firstly at a domestic level and then within the chapel. An elder said to me afterwards that their arguments against the right of women to speak or pray were based on shaky views of scripture. Their motivation had been prompted by a fear that if you gave women an inch they would end up running the chapel. And that applies to the wider problem.

Outcomes

When I retired to another part of Essex I was pleased to discover that the local Gospel Hall had a preaching elder who was a woman. This hall was of the same denomination as the first. I understand that many of these kinds of chapel came into more liberty in the Holy Spirit. That is not to say that the Holy Spirit's presence was entirely absent beforehand. It had, however, been overshadowed by lots of sincere intellectualism, and male dominance.

One leader of the first chapel was a great thinker and was widely known and respected. He was also a pragmatist. He was also patriarchal, a rich and generous person, and a poet. He was, from time to time, called upon to advise smaller chapels about their spiritual and material problems. Not surprisingly, the little chapel of two men and eighteen women had to send for him. One of the men had died and they were facing closure. The prospect was that the hall would have to be sold, and the Muslim community was keen to buy it.

I think my Muslim friends will understand there was no antipathy towards Islam when I say that that these Christians were upset to think that their meeting place of a hundred years might become a mosque. Their leader advised that the solution was for the eighteen women to take over the reins, preach the gospel, and perform all the management functions that had hitherto been the sole province of men.

A woman's dilemma

As the first chapel came into more freedom one of its male members became unhappy especially as his wife was of a different opinion. Now these people were known as Christian Brethren, and sometimes referred to as Open Brethren in order to distinguish them from Exclusive (or Close) Brethren. The latter were more austere and held independent views about end time's prophecy. About this time the latter became more extreme, adopting teaching about separation. If one was not "separated" they could not eat meals with them or sit in the same part of the chapel. This developed into situations in which members of the same family could not eat at the same table.

The wife of the man who dissented from the newfound freedom at the first chapel wrote to me in confidence and asked for an explanation of the single verse about women's silence. I wrote along the lines that I have already set out. From her answer I could tell she was in complete agreement with me. Sadly, her husband had taken drastic action. He had removed himself, his wife and children from the chapel and joined the exclusive set. For the sake of family unity she decided to submit to his opinions while holding in her heart a love of the truth. She would have to remain silent.

A blessed reversal

Another chapel of Exclusive Brethren became indoctrinated with these strange views of separation. Half of the members would not agree and so they left and founded a chapel of their own. They became known as the "outs" while the incumbents were called the "ins". A little while after this one of the "outs" realised that he owned the deeds of the original chapel and he was able to retake possession of it. Thereafter the "outs" became the "ins" and the "ins" became the "outs".

A sudden release

I did what I could to encourage able women from the Brethren. On two separate occasions when I was preaching in churches of other denominations I invited two different women to give short personal testimonies. They rose to the occasion magnificently but managed to emulate a filibuster. Instead of taking the fifteen minutes allocated they talked until the close of the meeting so I was unable to preach at all! It is very important not to blame these people because they were women. A man tried to do the same on another occasion. I had asked him to bring the scripture reading and chair the meeting. I would preach for half an hour. As he had left his glasses at home I had to bring the reading. He then proceeded to waffle about trivial things and then announced that I was going to sing. This is something I can't do! It was then that I had to take control of matters.

I will record briefly in another chapter how some women have not altogether helped Christian witness by pursuing flamboyant ministries. I must make it abundantly clear that there have been more men than women who have followed such a path. This is because there are more men in ministry than there are women and not because men are necessarily more exhibitionist. It is simply that this book is about women and the appalling deal that has been handed to them by men over centuries. The two women that crowded me out did so because they were like horses let out of a stable. It was a heady experience for them.

At the time that I am writing about, the Christian Brethren answered to the description of "sober", and that is part of the Christian make-up. Putting it another way, they were not, overtly, demonstrative. As they were so adamant about the need to take a single scripture in isolation from 1 Timothy, 2.11 by which to condemn countless women to silence, why did they not take another single verse from the same chapter and act upon that as well? "I will therefore that men pray everywhere, lifting up holy hands."

Evangelical objections

Many evangelical ministers believe that men have a "headship" role in the Church. Their objections to the equality of women in the Church, if they are to be validated, must be based on scripture. Unlike orthodox clergy, they cannot rest upon tradition, circumstantial evidence, or sacramental rites to bolster their case. The current attitude of both camps, orthodox and evangelical, seems to be based on determination to resist women's rights to the very end. For instance they have seized on the wording of the recent Synod vote, to set in motion a process to appoint women bishops, as providing future opportunity to overthrow the process before it becomes fully operative. They believe respectively that scripture and tradition are on their side. In the event of the appointment of women to bishoprics they are calling for extra "peripatetic" male bishops in their diocese. This is little short of insulting to a woman. What if women behaved in the same manner?

Chapter Six

AUTHORITY OF MEN

> "But I do not allow a woman to teach or usurp authority over a man." 2 Timothy. 2:12

Proliferation of views

Was it ever in the mind of God that women should be subjugated in his Church? Strong cases are made by men based on Biblical argument that they have an inalienable right to supremacy in the ministry. However, the position of women has improved in some denominations to such an extent that they have a right to equality. In general, the enjoyment of such a right is a long way from being a universal realisation. In some denominations they are still only on the first rung of an ecclesiastical ladder. Yet in others they cannot aspire to ordination at all. Some Anglican bishops interpret the scripture quoted above as preventing women from becoming bishops, and there is an ongoing debate in which there are two fairly entrenched sides.

A tough debate

As a champion of women's rights I must be careful not to fall into the same trap as misogynists. I very nearly did so. I must not strive, like they do, to make a case merely out of partisanship. That is to start from a preconceived notion and work one's way towards proving it. I must be confident of having a cast iron case by careful examination and be able to present it with conviction. That is not going to be easy. I must examine and contradict claims that are based on custom, tradition, culture, and interpretations of some scriptures. Before doing so I will re-emphasise my case based on the epistle to the Galatians. A case I have already discussed in the opening chapter. In God's estimate there is no difference between Jew or Greek, slave or free man, male or female: all are one in Christ Jesus. All are sons of God through faith in Christ Jesus. All are made new creatures by the power of the Spirit. These verses are unequivocal and must stand. This calls for a reappraisal of other scriptures that appear to mean on the face of them that there is a difference between the standing of men and women.

In addition to drawing attention to the strong teaching in the epistle to the Galatians I have also given instances in which God gave women authority and gifts of teaching in the past. Protagonists counter by arguing that the number of cases in which God used men, heavily outnumber the occasions when He called women. They rest heavily on the scripture quoted at the head of this chapter. They show no understanding of God's impartiality as opposed to the world's clamour for equality of numbers regardless of suitability for a particular type of work.

The source of authority

When Jesus gave his great commission to the Church he said that all authority had been given to him in heaven and on earth. The Authorised Version (AV) translates the word authority as *power* and that is because the two words are close in meaning. In original transcripts the word is *excousia* and Young's AV Concordance prefers *authority* as does the scholarly New American Standard Bible and the New International Version. So do the Catholic Ronald Knox and Jerusalem bibles. The source of present-day authority stems from the ascension of the triumphant Lord. Now, some would have it that Jesus devolved His authority exclusively on men because his words were addressed to the eleven apostles: he was starting a form of sexual apartheid.

I cannot accept such a contention and must, therefore, seek to find an explanation of *suffer not a woman* that will not vie with other positive scriptures I have already set out. Before doing this I must re-emphasise that *excousia* can mean power as well as authority and that another word for power is *dunamis* . Although Jesus told the eleven that all power was given to Him they did not receive the power at that very moment. He told them to tarry in Jerusalem until they were endued with power from high. When this power fell at Pentecost, women received it as well as men.

Apostolic teaching

Although Paul's letters can be taken as authentic it does not follow that every instruction contained in these should be applied rigidly to each following generation. Paul was aware of this and made it clear that in places there were differing degrees of importance in his various teachings, and even an exception in one place. He also wrote about problems peculiar to the Church he was addressing. The Corinthian Church was immature in its worship and wayward in its morals. Nevertheless, his teaching about the conduct of worship, particularly as far as spiritual gifts are concerned in the twelfth, thirteenth, and fourteenth chapters of his first letter, became a model. However, some of those who place emphasis upon scriptures they think support a preference for men, also think that spiritual gifts have ceased (or at the least inspirational gifts), not recognising that Paul's teaching on gifts of the spirit is for today. That is all of his teaching on this subject. This is especially important to the role of men and women as kings and priests.

The eleventh chapter of Paul's first epistle to the Corinthians is a major debating ground for protagonists who favour man's headship over women. Yet a close examination shows that in this matter Paul is in the field of tradition (see Authorised Version verse 2, "ordinances" "or traditions". These were given orally at Corinth or possibly written in the lost letter – see critical notes of the late Rev Canon Evans, Professor of Greek, University of Durham. This verse is sanitised in the NIV by reference to "teachings" only). His following obscure remarks about head-covering and shaving the head are taken by hardly anybody to relate to present-day deportment. He states, in verse 8, that a woman ought to have a symbol of authority on her head because of the angels: whatever that was supposed to mean in his day. It has no relevance to us. Moving into spiritual matters he writes in verse 11: "however, in the Lord (note "in the Lord") neither is woman independent of the man, nor is man independent of the woman". There we have God's splendid impartiality! This is strengthened in verse 12 where Paul writes that although woman originated from man, every man is born of a woman.In Peter's first epistle we can find at the beginning of Chapter Three an instruction for women to be submissive to their husbands and this is in order to be good witnesses to disobedient men. He appears to be addressing a situation where women were better Christians than their husbands. In order to make it clear that men and women were equal spiritually before God

Peter wrote in verse 7 that men should honour women as heirs of the grace of life. Why? It was so that their prayers would not be hindered.

About female head covering, the culture of the time influenced his requirement for a more substantial veil or shawl than the hat adopted in Victorian England. A hat is deemed to be outmoded and ostentatious within non-orthodox churches. Jewish converted men probably kept their hats on in the early Church. God was satisfied with this practice throughout the Old Testament. What man would dare keep a hat on in church today: only if he was a bald boy! The submission of women to men may also have been a practice that was carried over from the temple. Behaviour patterns may have been important and proprietary according to custom and culture.

Paul's instruction about remembering the Lord's death did not come from him. He received this from the Lord as a revelation and made it clear that it was binding and, therefore, it was also for posterity. His other instructions were based on personal opinion. In one instance instructions about conduct of believers who had been married prior to conversion depended upon whether their partner was a believer or not.

Some would have been married to two wives at the same time. About celibacy this was a concession, not a command. His command to divorcees not to remarry was his own and not the Lord's. In fact these were at variance with the Lord's own teaching that allowed remarriage of innocent parties in cases of adultery. By implication an innocent party could marry because under the old covenant an adulterer was stoned to death. He wrote about non-believing partners making it clear that the views were his own not the Lord's. If a non-believer wished to abandon a marriage he or she was free to do so.

As to a woman not teaching or usurping authority over a man, I have shown that women were equal in other instances. Surely, Paul was addressing a local problem. Were women at Corinth ignoring the leading of the Holy Spirit? At Thyatira a woman was called *Jezebel* by the risen Lord. There was another instance when two women were at loggerheads in a belligerent way.

Two-way communications

Paul's letters left so much with us that teaches and instructs the Church today. In another chapter I shall write about the vital teaching on the priesthood. His letters were not written out of the blue. Churches would write to him for advice and there was a to and fro passage of assistants like Stephanus, Fortunatus, and Achaicus. Helpers carried gifts from one church to another. There were many ways in which Paul gathered information as to how churches were doing. He wrote into local situations he had been alerted to.

That is why Paul sometimes gave advice or made it clear that solutions were based on his own judgment. *Suffer not a woman* may well have been written about a particular woman in Timothy's church. As to a woman not being able to teach, again, we know that at *Thyatira* a woman was a false teacher who led people into immoral acts. Only very wealthy women would be educated and very few would have a deep knowledge of the scriptures like Lois and Priscilla who both taught men.

Culture

People in the early Church, including Paul, were creatures of the culture of the day except that they eschewed what was sinful. So are we! In the last century in Wales a man would have been sent to Coventry if he went out without a hat on. Other men would have refused to walk with him. It was improper to attend a meeting wearing a suit without a waistcoat. Early Christians were influenced by Jewish, Roman and Greek culture. Men were the breadwinners. Women reared children. Male physical strength was all important in terms of fighting wars, building and hewing. The fact that most of Paul's associate ministers were men and that he wrote to *men* and to *brothers* is symptomatic of the times he lived in rather than of God's perfect order.

As I mentioned in the Preface, when Paul wrote about the headship of a man he was referring to a man's headship of the family according to tradition (or ordinances). This makes arguments about the meaning of *kephale* inconsequential. In the same chapter it is made clear that in family prayers men and women are equal before God. We make a mistake in thinking that there is such a thing as a perfect child of Adam. The Great Apostle was one of a few who were conscious of their carnal old natures. He was so privileged by his revelations and exceptional gifting that a great fear of becoming conceited came upon him. He realised that his thorn in the flesh was to prevent him from becoming puffed up. No one is good except God. It is only with this in mind that I dare to suggest that Paul had an opinion of women that was influenced by the times he lived in. He had been married because that was a qualification for being a member of the Sanhedrin. We know he was not in a married state when he served the Lord. He makes no mention of his wife which leads me to suppose that she was alive but not living with him. His comments about head coverings and a woman shaving her head can only have related to custom. Can anyone explain what this had to do with angels?

Under the Law of Moses the children of Israel did not eat animals with cloven hooves such as pigs. Yet God gave Peter a vision of such animals being lowered down in a net. He was not to regard what God had made as unclean. So what applied under the Law of Moses did not so apply in the New Testament. There was a difference between the cultures of the old and the new dispensations. Moses allowed men to have two wives because of their hardness of heart. This was contrary to the teaching of Jesus. There is also a difference between what is not permissible in human society and the liberty that there is in Christ. Sometimes the formers' prohibitions inhibits the latter's expansiveness.

On the other hand society in democratic countries has, largely, been much kinder to women than have the bulk of Christian leaders.

Tradition

By tradition the man is the head of the family and as regards decision-making is the boss. Women should be subject to their husbands. This is a convention that does not hold up in reality in the present day. Even where it applies it is based on earthly principles. There is merit in the teaching so long as the husband's charge of loving his wife is also upheld. It is sad that today not many men give up a seat on a train to a woman. Now this is an unfortunate development of human culture. It is a sign of increasing selfishness and lack of consideration for others. In the spiritual realm things are different. It is true, notionally, that those who are in Christ are equal and free from the law of sin and death. But instead of this freedom leading to licentiousness, the love of Christ constrains them to be like him. Perfect love casts out fear. We no longer argue about who is king of the castle. We consider others to be better than us. We serve and the one that would be great must be the servant of all. There is no such principle to be found in tradition.

There are two kingdoms, one of which is the kingdom of this world. We live in it and must abide by its rules. Otherwise there would be anarchy. There must be authority. Paul teaches in the thirteenth chapter of his letter to the Romans that every soul is subject to the higher powers. The powers that be are ordained of God. It is in such an ethos that women have been regarded as the weaker sex and less privileged sex.

The world is changing. Battles are fought by pressing buttons. In the Western world women have been emancipated politically for about a hundred years. They have equal access to education, and have all the benefits of technology in their daily lives. They drive cars, fly aircraft, and sail round the world on their own. As far as women are concerned the world is giving them equal status at a faster rate than is being afforded to them in the Church. The broad Church, therefore, is dragging its feet on two counts. It can no longer hide behind the excuse of having to conform to cultural mores in the treatment of women and it is not rightly interpreting God's rule of impartiality. It is resisting the Holy Spirit.

Women priests

If I was asked whether women should be priests I would give a shock answer: no, they should not. I would qualify my reply by saying that neither should men and add that I was only referring to the most generally accepted meaning of the word priest. The subject of priesthood needs to be rehearsed thoroughly before its relationship to the ministry of women can be clarified. In the following chapters I will explain the differences between: Melchisedec the Priest; The Aaronic Priesthood; Jesus the Great High Priest; and both men and women as kings and priests to God, or the priesthood of all believers.

Once different kinds of priests are identified and their status is understood people will be able to judge for themselves in which instances there is still a need for priests, and whether there are other instances in which the very notion of priesthood is redundant. In these latter cases it appears that a decision to perpetuate an order of priests was not founded on scripture. It was a question of human teaching, well into the first millennium, that the Mosaic Law could be adapted and introduced into a new covenant. This decision has a huge bearing on the present-day controversy about women priests in both Orthodoxy and the Anglican Church.

A caveat

I am not suggesting that different forms of worship are always inappropriate. Presbyters were first called "priests" by Lucian in the second century. Spiritual innovations were made in the third century when a sacerdotal mass was introduced by Cyprian. The mass became a daily ritual in AD 394. The celibacy of priests was declared in AD 1079. All these developments were founded on intellectual reasoning. However, when Pope Innocent III defined Transubstantiation in AD 1215, this amounted to a serious departure from scripture. Spiritual truths were replaced by teaching that Jesus was literally and physically present in the emblems of bread and wine (the Council of Trent declared that those who did not believe this were cursed) and this resulted in a practice of locking up what was claimed to be Jesus in metal tabernacles on earthly altars by a re-instituted privileged male priesthood. The Church of England Series 3 Communion appears to give worshippers two options. Communion can be regarded as purely spiritual, with which I have no quarrel, or it can be seen as a quasi-Roman-Catholic-type Eucharist. The latter option is a departure from scripture and a main cause of objections to the ordination of women. This amounts to a fudge, and I am unhappy about it. (See: Appendix 3.)

Chapter Seven

ABRAHAM: THE SPIRIT OF FAITH

> "And Melchisedec the King of Salem brought out bread and wine; now he was a priest of God Most High." Genesis 14:18

A long journey

This chapter heralds the beginning of a long spiritual journey in which God gradually brought his children into fuller light regarding his perfect will.

The spirit preceded the law

With Abraham came the beginning of faith. This is a precious gift that will never be annulled. It is a highly personal link with God. As such it has transcended all that history could throw at it. It is epitomised in this chapter by an encounter between Abraham and Melchisedec because this king had no end, and was, or is a type of Christ our great High Priest. This faith can be exercised by men and women alike, and so in spirit, if not in worldly life, women have been regarded by God as equals from virtually the beginning of time. I must trace the worldly reality of events in order to show how men overlooked women in their relationship with God, and how God made this known. The extent to which men heeded Him, or did not, is the burden of my book.

Melchisedec was the first priest ever mentioned in the Bible. He is shrouded in mystery, and as far as the Old Testament is concerned particularly so. This only reveals that he was both a king and a priest. He blessed Abram after the latter defeated Chedorlaomer and a number of kings. Abram gave him a tenth of all. The most telling things about this priest are: that he belonged to an order of priesthood that preceded the Aaronic priesthood by 400 years; he was not of the tribe of Levi (in fact the tribes did not exist); and he did not sacrifice animals. He brought out bread and wine.

Fortunately we can glean more about him from the Book of Hebrews. His name could be translated King of Righteousness, and also King of Salem, which is King of Peace. He had no father or mother; was without genealogy, having neither beginning of days nor end of life. Being made like the Son of God, he abides a priest perpetually. Perhaps I should be content to accept this without speculation. Unfortunately, I am a trained investigator and analyst, so bear with me. The whole episode could have been a pre-incarnate appearance of Jesus himself; it could have been a divinely inspired vision, or there may be such priests in heaven. In support of the view that it was the Lord himself is another account of the Lord appearing to Abraham on the plains of Mamre. God the Father would not appear as a person. God is a spirit. The Father, the first person of the trinity, spoke to Moses from a burning bush. He did not appear as a material being.

The supernatural

In order to begin to appreciate the appearance of Melchisedec on the earthly scene one must understand that it was an event beyond natural laws. We are looking at the realm of the supernatural. It is highly spiritual. Many theologians will not submit to a concept of miracles. Accounts of walking on water, changing water into wine, raising the dead, and multiplying loaves are derided. But my case for the recognition of women without fear or favour rests on the spiritual character of God's kingdom which is in the sphere of the invisible. The things that are seen are temporal but the things that are not seen are eternal. It is only in the spiritual realm that there is no difference between male and female. This is God's realm and it impacted on a fallen world very gradually. God had a plan of redemption, but mankind had to wait for it to unfold. The phenomenon of Melchisedec was a very early sign of God's grace to a fallen humanity.

God's heavenly markers

That encounter between Abram and Melchisedec was a manifestation of God's graciousness. It was a sign or marker of how redemption would be brought about. After the fall of mankind an immediate promise was given that a Messiah would bruise the serpent's head. We are told that sin entered into the world, and death through sin. Spiritual death reigned from Adam until Moses, and this is the period Abraham lived in. Earlier, Enoch had walked with God and went to be with him; presumably without going through death. Signs of God's intervention emerged; as to righteousness, a promise that Abraham would become the father of two great nations, and of Isaac the child of promise, as to unrighteousness, the destruction of Sodom. These events were milestones on a long path. This path was also littered with displays of man's inclination to sow to the flesh. Thus there was Abraham's supreme faith and obedience, and his deviousness in Egypt and impatience in consorting with Hagar. However, God continued to endure the contradiction of sinners against Himself. At the same time he encouraged people by acts of divine power and awesome encounters.

The Father's long-suffering

A loving father will never force his children to follow what he knows to be the best for them. He gives them their heads, partly because they will learn from their mistakes, and partly because he wishes to retain their love. Abraham received promises from God and although he believed them he was over anxious about fulfilment. First of all since Abraham had no offspring, he purposed to make Eleazer his heir, because he was born in his household. God would not allow this. Abraham then resorted to having a son by Hagar. He should have waited until God's purpose was fulfilled in the way that was intended. Sarah was to bear Isaac. A long time after this Habakkuk prophesied that the vision was for the appointed time; it hastens towards the goal and it will not fail. Though it tarries, wait for it; for it will certainly come.

The vision of the emancipation of women would become possible through the ministry of Jesus who was of the order of Melchisedec. A long period under the law would intervene followed by centuries of frustration. Man would devise ways in which to circumvent God's real intentions. Women could become nuns; a service which was both inferior and subject to "priests" who were the outcome of an adapted, perpetual pattern of the Aaronic priesthood.

Contrasts

Under Moses Israel was to become subject to a ceremonial law in which tangible objects, (e.g. paraphernalia like lamps, carved objects and brazen lavers) were used in tent meetings. These objects were shadows of something better that was to come. I will explain in the next chapter both the temporal significance of such instruments of worship, and how these were superseded by spiritual realities. I have already mentioned that men in the new post-mosaic covenant, in which we live today, mistakenly perpetuated the ceremonial law, with modified overtones. These are seemingly oblivious to the significance of Melchisedec, and of the appearing of Jesus, who is a high priest according to the order of this mysterious man. The epistle to the Hebrews painstakingly explains the superiority of the spiritual by pointing out that Levi (as serving the law) could be said to have paid tithes to Melchisedec. When Abram paid tithes to this King of Salem, Levi was not yet born, but in his great grandfather's loins. Putting it in a more simple way, Levi (representing the Aaronic priesthood) was of the earth earthy, whereas Melchisedec was of the heavenly realm. Aaron was the first high priest of the Mosaic law. Aaron was the second son of Levi and Moses was his brother. They all died and thus ceased to be priests. Melchisedec had no beginning and no end. Hence Jesus was a priest forever; that is not on the basis of a law of physical requirement, but according to the power of an indestructible life.

Women did not serve at the tent of meeting or later in the temple. Sons of the tribe of Levi had two unique privileges. Aaron's descendants were anointed priests who conducted sacrifices and other ceremonial functions; all the other Levites were responsible for looking after the trappings. They assembled the tent of meeting, dismantled it, transported it, and maintained it. Present-day priests who perform Eucharistic rites are seen as being akin to Aaron's progeny. Altar servers are seen as akin to ordinary Levites. There was no such thing as an altar girl in orthodoxy for two millennia. Within the last two decades girls have served on the altar in some English parishes. This is probably because there are shortages of willing boys! Necessity can override all kinds of objections. This is one of several recent changes of attitude towards females that I have been alerted to. I will return to these developments in Part II.

Abramic Covenant

Abraham believed God and it was counted to him as righteousness. In this we can see the dawn of an eternal future for mankind. Although death reigned through sin, in its midst, a pulse of faith began to beat. God approached Abram who came from a family of idol-worshippers and told him to leave his home, in Haran, and to go forth, not knowing where God's intended destination for him would be. He went out in faith, in obedience, looking for a city whose maker and builder was God. He was seventy-five years of age. Sara his wife and Lot his nephew went with him and they took all their possessions. He passed through the land of Canaan. God promised Abram that his descendants would be given this land. He went forth again and arrived in Egypt. After journeying through the Negev he returned to the land God had promised to him. He dwelt in the oaks of Mamre, which are in Hebron.

It is important to note this covenant was certain because of faith in God's promise. It is exactly the same faith as authentic Christian believers exercise to day. The, then, covenant was incomplete because sin reigned and there was no remedy. Today, under the free covenant, faith can know that the remedy has been applied. A great high priest has offered a one true sacrifice for sin.

Comparing covenants

In successive chapters I will be covering the nature and meaning of three covenants. I have already explained much about the first-mentioned Abrahamic covenant. I will show that the second-mentioned covenant of the Law was almost like a step backward when examined from a spiritual standpoint. It was only a shadow of what was to come in the new (third-mentioned) covenant. That is one still of faith but sealed in the blood of Jesus. Why then did Israel go through so many years of legalism; of works; of prohibitions? Well, not only did it have to learn about itself, also its experiences were to be a lesson for us. They said to God, "we will do everything you say." That was absolute nonsense. They did not understand God's gift of righteousness but set about to establish their own.

In setting out a detailed pattern of communion and of moral behaviour in a codified law it could be shown how far short the people were falling. By introducing feasts, sacrifices, and symbols of a temporal nature it could be seen in retrospect that these foreshadowed a covenant of grace; the coming of unseen spiritual things; a realm that would make the past completely obsolete. The law of the second covenant was ineffectual. The killing of bulls and goats did not save the people. But the kind of faith started in the first covenant (and possessed by some in the second) was effectual. Thus Melchisedec was more effective than Aaron. My key point here is that the first covenant manifested the first shoots of equality of all, whereas the second covenant was one of bondage in which women did not figure. The second covenant is artificially perpetuated within orthodox religion and there is no place for women amongst its ordinands.

Isaac

Isaac was a child of promise, born of a seemingly barren woman in her old age. He was the first-born of a line from which the Messiah would emerge. By character he was meek. His enemies reckoned he was weak and were dumbfounded when this man, who gave in rather than being contentious, finished up with greater flocks and riches than any of them. The story of his wells provides a lesson to us. We need not strive. With God on our side there is strength in weakness as defined by the world.

A number of Abraham's wells had been filled up by others and had fallen into disuse. As Isaac then cleared these and the water flowed again his enemies wanted them back. He gave in and finally dug a super well which he shared. The penultimate well was named Rehoboth by Isaac because he said, "The Lord has made room for us and we shall be fruitful in the land." He and Rebeka were, indeed, blessed. Their characters and natures were pleasing to God. After all they epitomised, albeit imperfectly, what he was planning to bring forth in a new creation. These would be people with a character that is Christ-like.

Ever since the world began women have not striven to any extent to be equal. Circumstances have not been in their favour. However, modern technology and growth of knowledge have now changed the field. Their lack of bellicosity and showing of gentleness will not have escaped divine notice. Not only are women rightfully equal as spiritually new creatures; their status is guaranteed in the world to come. At the judgment gender will be inconsequential as will be one's denomination. If people are not afforded the ministry they are capable of then it is a great loss to the Church. If people are less gifted but try to do their best then the Holy Spirit can make up any deficiency.

Jacob

This is a man whose name was changed to Israel. His twin brother Esau was born first. It was written that the older would serve the younger. This turned out to be the case physically. The words also have a deep spiritual meaning for us. After a spiritual rebirth the sinful former nature remains. It was said that as Isaac was delivered he had hold of his brother's heel. If we liken Esau as representing the sinful nature and Jacob the new nature then there is a simile. The sinful nature exists first and can be deemed the older. The new nature follows at conversion. These two natures in a child of God are contrary, one to the other. The flesh and the spirit fight. The Spirit will overcome.

Jacob became the Patriarch of Israel, his sons becoming the heads of the tribes. Levi became the head of the tribe that inherited the priestly and diaconate functions of the ceremonial law. Judah became the head of the line from which the Messiah would emerge. Well did the prophet say that Bethlehem in the land of Judah will not be least in among the princes of Judah for out of it would come forth a ruler who would rule God's people: Israel. Even Herod's advisors were in no doubt that this prophecy related to the expected Messiah. It is relevant to my main study that Mary was of the line of Judah and that she was descended from David. It is her genealogy that is provided in the first chapter of Matthew's gospel. As a mark of the divine inclusiveness there are two gentile women in that tree: Ruth the Moabitess and Rahab the Harlot. For some strange reason Paul left out the name of Deborah from his list of faithful champions in Hebrews, Chapter Eleven. He included the name of Rahab. But who am I to raise a query?

The law

Jacob's grandsons, Moses and Aaron, were instrumental, under God, in bringing in a ceremonial law. This had its place in the divine calendar as will emerge in the next chapter. To go through every jot and tittle would be boring in the context of women's rights. However, the salient features will be seen primarily, as always pointing fascinatingly towards a future understanding of the truth of freedom in Christ. As viewed on the ground, however, these merely reinforce a fact that there was a complete absence of recognition of women's rightful role in service and worship.

Chapter Eight

MOSES AND AARON: THE LAW

> "Now these are the ordinances you shall set before them."
> Exodus 21:1

Why this chapter?

This chapter is not just a matter of padding out. Indeed it is critical to my case for women. If this is not immediately apparent, please bear with me. I have already emphasised the importance of faith in the development of God's dealing with humanity, and postulated that Abraham's faith was a first spark leading to the prospective, eventual, freedom of all who exercise faith in Christ. Although the law proved to be a retrograde step, there were good reasons for its introduction. Israel had told God that they would do everything He said. So he let them get on with it. They had to learn that their own righteousness would not get them anywhere. The most fascinating and challenging thing about the ordinances of the law and its set feasts is that, unknown to Israel, they were placed in their sacred calendar by God so that these would synchronise with the literal days and dates of the death, burial and resurrection of Jesus. That in itself is enough to surprise an unbeliever. However, of even greater importance is the unerring relationship between the events in these two calendars (that is: the sacred and the eternal) which place in juxtaposition the covenants of law and of grace.

By describing the main Jewish ordinances and feasts and aligning these with days and events in the first and second comings of Christ, I have sought to show a progression leading prospectively from regimes of harsh legality to enjoyments of equal privileges between men and women in the Church. The goal would be to base leadership decisions on the principles of divine impartiality.

The next best thing

I need to describe the manner in which God set out a mode of conduct for the people of Israel through his servant Moses for them to follow. The period from the giving of the law on Mount Sinai until the coming of the Messiah would cover about 1,270 years. I am concerned with recounting the position of women or, rather, the lack of it during this period. Details of the political fortunes and misfortunes of what was firstly a theocracy, and then successively, captivity, a return, and finally a Roman occupation are very instructive. I have already mentioned the Patriarchs and it will be sufficient here if I briefly remind readers of the historic experiences of Israel under the law.

There was the Exodus from Egypt, wandering in the wilderness, the conquest of Canaan, the Amphictomy (the period of the Judges), the Monarchy, Independent Kingdoms of Israel and Judah, Assyrian Conquest, the end of Assyrian domination, the Exilic and Postexilic periods, restoration, the completion of the second temple, reforms of Nehemiah and Ezra, the Jews under the Ptolemies, Seleucid Conquest, profanation of the Temple, Rededication of the Temple.

I will deal with the continuation of the Jewish religion throughout this period, especially as far as the law and the feasts were concerned. I will try to adopt an understanding and sympathetic approach and to show that the law was not some monster of morbidity as some have painted it, including some of the early Fathers. The spirit had not been universally given. There was a need to bring a people ultimately to a greater destiny; to try them, and to rule them. I will not label the period of the law as perfect, but suggest that it was the next best thing to that which was to come in the future.

Not just an automaton

Very late in the law period, especially as far as the Pharisees were concerned, there was an excessive attention to detail. There was a danger of automatic conformity, although this may not have been the intention. All along, rabbis had encouraged people to love God and their neighbour, to be forgiving, to give alms, and follow after being righteous. The ordinances were seen as everlasting. That is that these did not begin with Moses. Psalm 119.160 states that every one of God's ordinances is everlasting. The Feast of Weeks was reckoned to be celebrated by Noah, and the Feast of Tabernacles by Abraham. However, I am inclined to think that they were stretching things a bit. I will show that there were things, such as the feasts, that were occasions of joy. God also came into the meeting place in a great, overpowering glory. That is until he became aggrieved and departed. There were other things about the law that are hard to understand. I expressed reservations about the continual slaughter of animals in my book *The Finger of God.* I will be giving other examples here that relate to women and the eating of animals.

Purification after childbirth

Under the law a woman was deemed to be unclean following childbirth and had to undergo a period of purification. In the book of Leviticus after the birth of a son a mother was ceremonially unclean for seven days. On the eighth day a boy is circumcised and a mother must wait a further thirty-three days before going to the sanctuary. It is puzzling that after the birth of a daughter the corresponding days are virtually doubled to fourteen and sixty-six. Some expositors prefer not to comment, finding the subject difficult. But the whole wonder of childbirth is mysterious.

The early Fathers (i.e: Church leaders in the post-apostolic period) had no qualms because they were misogynists. Women, they said, were equal to the lower side of human nature. They were the first to fall into temptation. The Fathers misused Paul's first letter to Timothy. Paul was stating a fact without being accusative. He even went on to say that a woman would be saved in child-bearing. Expositors tend to agree this did not mean a literal salvation but probably a nullifying of ceremonial obligations under a newer and better covenant.

As to the real reason for the adoption of days of purification under the ceremonial law: Hindus, Brahmins, Parsees, Arabs (according to Burckhardt), and Greeks all adopted similar customs relating to childbirth. They all adopted a period of forty days. So it was a general custom in the world at large. What is more interesting is that, in the clinical realm, men such as Hippocrates and Aristotle believed that a mother suffered for a longer time after the birth of a daughter, which shows the whole matter in a non-condemnatory light. It does not matter that modern medicine finds no proof of this. It was what was generally believed and presents us with a much more acceptable explanation as far as respect for women is concerned.

The Ten Commandments were given to Moses by God and stand for ever. It cannot be said that many of the details of the ceremonial law were more than rules relating to health and hygiene and the physical well-being of Israel. For instance, the law relating to the selection, and eating of animals seems to have been based on assessments of which would furnish the best and most wholesome meal. There are parallel distinctions in Islam and Hinduism. When Peter was about to be called as a missionary to the gentiles he was given a vision of a net being lowered full of what would have been prohibited animals, and told to eat them. God told him that he was not to regard what he had made as being unclean. So here was a clear alteration from the Mosaic Law espoused by God under a new and better covenant. To those of us who baulk at the former Jewish practice of sacrificing animals there is the consolation that Jesus said he would not have sacrifice but obedience. Also inexplicably, as far as human wisdom is involved, the Jews stopped slaughtering animals after the destruction of the Temple. They did not understand the real reason for cessation, which was that there had been a one and only perfect sacrifice on a cross thus making the law obsolete.

Absence of women

In the law period women were excluded from carrying out priestly and other Levite duties. We know, late in the period, that women served in the second temple, but this was a service of prayer and fasting, something like the service of nuns today. In fact it is this very similarity that I seize upon to show why women are not afforded their full rights in orthodoxy. The traditional absence of women in old law ceremonial has been carried forward into the New Testament by major Christian denominations despite the fact that the Aaronic priesthood became obsolete. With respect, this does not apply to the order of Melchisedec of which Jesus is a great high priest. I will develop my case in the next chapter.

The feasts

A number of feasts were kept under the Law of Moses. These were either joyful or solemn occasions. They were for all the people so women would have participated and undoubtedly played an active role at least in the joyful kind. I can imagine Ruth and Naomi being involved in First Fruits and Harvest! Many Western Christian denominations today lack aspects of joy and celebration, probably on account of national characteristics of suppressed decorum. The wonderful thing about these feasts is that these foreshadowed critical events that were to take place in the divine calendar as I will explain. The reason I am taking readers through all these festivities is to show them that they typified future divine events that were to bring in the days of God's impartiality as to gender, rather than using these as proofs of female exclusion as misogynists are apt to do.

There were six principal feasts in the Jewish sacred calendar, as opposed to their civic calendar. All these feasts were given to Israel, but every gentile was included so there was equality. Because every stage of redemption is typified by these feasts it follows that a future freedom in Christ was being shadowed or pointed to.

The Passover

This celebrates the night upon which the Jews conducted their exodus from Egypt. A lamb was taken and killed by each household and its blood sprinkled on the doorposts. When the angel of death came to slay the first-born of Egypt he saw the blood and passed over. The New Testament contains clear teaching that links this feast with the death of Christ, *"For Christ our Passover has been sacrificed" (1 Corinthians 5:7).* In orthodoxy there is the magnificent singing of the Agnus Dei (Lamb of God). To demonstrate that the calendar of redemption was mysteriously linked by actual dates with the related Jewish feasts I will give an example. Jesus went up to the Feast of Tabernacles six months before the Passover. At first He was reluctant to go saying His time was not yet come. He changed His mind and went, speaking out boldly. We are told that no man laid hands on Him because His hour was not yet come. We know that Jesus died at the Passover! Therefore He could not in God's purpose have been killed at the Feast of Tabernacles. Even more remarkable is that according to John 13:1, before the feast of the Passover Jesus knew that His hour was come. He knew that He should depart out of this world unto the Father having loved His own which were in the world. He loved them to the end.

Unleavened bread

This feast was held on the fifteenth day of the month and lasted for seven days. Leaven is a type of sin and the Jews scrupulously put even the least scrap of leaven out of their houses. I am sure the women did this. It was set for the next day after Passover. Unleavened bread was a type of the sinless body of Christ. His body was laid in the tomb on the day after the Passover pending His resurrection. This exactly followed the Jewish sacred calendar.

First fruits

The priests took a sheaf of the first fruits and laid it before the Lord. It was called a wave offering. It was only the first of the "first fruits". A complete ingathering was to follow. This was representative of Christ as the bread of life in a spiritual sense. *"It is the spirit that quickened. The flesh profits nothing."* John: 6.63. Here we have, firstly, the thought of Christ being the first fruits as representing initial conversion in which we pass from death to life, and, secondly, a hope of final physical resurrection. That is why there was a distinction between the wave offering and the complete ingathering. This is quite remarkable.

The priest waved the offering vigorously for a long time while the people praised God. There was nothing solemn. It was a time of adoration and joy. The Kingdom of God is righteousness, peace and joy in the Holy Spirit. Paul wrote, now is Christ risen from the dead and become the first fruits of them that slept. The date of this feast was on the morning after the Jewish Sabbath which was the first day of the week. Believers are Easter people!

The importance of this feast to our study is that our spiritual resurrection is the point at which we become one in Christ. There is no longer any difference between male and female.

Pentecost

Or Feast of Weeks. After the First Fruits, celebrated at the barley harvest, the Jews numbered fifty days and offered a new meat offering. This was brought from houses and consisted of two wave loaves of fine flour, baked with leaven. This was Pentecost and came at the wheat harvest. It is representative of the great harvest as a result of the Christian Pentecost.

Remarkably, Pentecost is fifty days after Christ's resurrection in the Christian calendar. Eventually, what a gathering, what a gathering, what a gathering of the ransomed there shall be! The loaves were huge. It was a time of joy. Freewill offerings were made to the Lord and according to the writer of the Book of Deuteronomy there was a generous spirit towards the Levites, the stranger, orphans and widows.

The Holy Spirit came upon 120 in the upper room as promised by the glorified Jesus. This would be fifty days after his resurrection. Et resurrexit tertia dei, secundum scripturas, et ascendit in caelum sedet adexteram Patris.

Trumpets

The times of the feasts so far covered match exactly the events surrounding the death and resurrection of Jesus. This feast and the other two following feasts were observed at the closing stages of the year. They spanned about three weeks. They correspond to the second coming. The blowing of trumpets had no connection with the blowing of the shofar at the secular Jewish New Year. Trumpets are to be blown, according to the Bible, at the taking up of the Church. There will be two in a field and one will be taken and one left. It is a mystery. We shall not all sleep, but we shall all be changed. In a moment, in the twinkling of an eye, at the last trump, and the dead shall be raised incorruptible.

Atonement

The Jews rank this as the most solemn of all the feasts. It relates to the saving of their souls by atonement for sins. The celebration indicates tribulation, or all who keep the feast must afflict their souls, and make an offering by fire to the Lord. This is a time of repentance and humbling. Anything eaten must be accompanied with bitter herbs.

The realm of prophecy is full of pitfalls. Most expositors agree this feast is not connected with the atonement of Christ. It is about the ultimate destiny of Israel: about a remnant being saved. Some will be cut off. It is thought to be connected with a great final tribulation. Surely, the Holocaust must figure in this as the time of Jacob's trouble. This is only a personal observation.

Tabernacles

The first day was a holy convocation. No servile work was to be done. It began on the first day of the week and lasted for seven days. They took the branches of trees, branches of palms, and boughs of willows, and made booths, and lived in them. It was reminiscent of when they came out of Egypt and lived in booths. They were not only remembering the past but also looking forward to the coming of the Messiah. This feast corresponds with the Bible prediction that God is to tabernacle with people at the end of history. They will be his people and he will be their God. There will be a new heaven and a new earth. We shall reign as kings and priests with Christ. This will be a priesthood of all believers (that is both men and women) offering sacrifices of praise. That is a continuation of an identically similar role that is intended in the present spiritual kingdom here on earth.

At the first advent of Jesus as related in John's Gospel we read that the Word (Jesus) was made flesh and dwelt amongst us, or literally "tabernacled" amongst people. The thought is that he was God in a body, or tent.

Instruments of worship

There were finite things used in the carrying out of the ceremonial law, such as tents, later the Temple, the holy place, the holy of holies, the Ark of the Covenant, the golden brazier, lamps, table, altar, censures, golden laver, and robes. These all had an unforeseen significance for the future new and eternal covenant. The essential difference was that under the law, material and visible temporal things were in use, whereas under spiritual freedom things would be unseen and eternal. The importance of these contrasts to my study is that under the first legal reign women took no part in the sacrificing ceremonies, and under the second reign women were in God's estimate freely admissible. I refute the argument of some that as women did not participate in worship under the law, neither should they at the present day. It has been overlooked that the very feasts and ordinances were pointing forward, mysteriously, to the advent of freedom in Christ.

The New Testament asserts that these instruments were an example of, and shadows of, heavenly things; they were the pattern of things in the heavens; and a shadow of good things to come (Hebrews 8, 9, and

10). Liberals state that there is no benefit to be had in studying the minute details of liturgical and ceremonial activities. If they mean that some place too much store on things like strands of goat hair, or tassels, I concede that they have a point. If they cannot see the wonder of the main things I am unfolding then I must conclude theirs is the myopic vision.

The legalists do not look beyond the events of the law but, unlike the liberals, place so much store on these that they perpetuate the bald principles to suit their own ends, namely by keeping people, particularly women, under their thumbs. It is anomalous that in orthodoxy a celibate male hierarchy should on the one hand venerate, a woman, the blessed and wonderful Virgin Mary, to a station nearly equal to God, yet deny all other women equal status with them in the Lord's service. It is only living mortal women that are seen as a threat to the continuation of male dominance.

The Tabernacle

This was considered to be of such importance that fifteen chapters are devoted to the divine instructions about its construction and manner of operation in the Book of Exodus. This was a structure divided into two compartments. In the largest section all the sacred duties were performed by the priests. This was the Holy Place. The smaller section was called the Holiest of All, or the Holy of Holies. It was here that the glory of God descended. It was here that the High Priest entered once a year on the Day of Atonement to sprinkle blood on the mercy seat. I will explain the connection between the Jewish tabernacle and Christianity in Chapter Nine.

My later explanations will include references to things in the Holy Place, namely: the table containing shewbread; the Golden Candlestick; and the Golden Altar. Likewise of things in the Holiest of All: the Ark; the Mercy Seat; and the Cherubims.

The Court of the Tabernacle

The outer court was a large area enclosed by curtains and consisted of: the Gate of the Court; the Brazen Altar; and the Brazen Laver. Those who attended were divided into three classes: the Priests, the Levites; and the Common People (the children of Israel). I will be discussing the significance of the physical rending of the curtain in the Temple on the death of Christ, and its spiritual significance as the middle wall of petition came down, and what portents this held for all believers.

People of habit

It is possible to be too quick in selecting an isolated scripture to support a preconceived end and to leave no room for weighing other relevant passages or to exercise wider wisdom. For example the scripture appearing to ban women from teaching men or of ever becoming bishops has conditioned attitudes in the Church. In Ezra's day when the word was re-examined and there was repentance it resulted in great blessing.

Over a very long period patterns of worship have been adopted that, generally, have been reverent, serious, solemn, stereotyped, and restrained. Unfortunately, whenever traditional modes have been broken there has been a tendency towards over-emotionalism, and even, more rarely, hysteria. The latter characteristics have resulted in an entrenched conservatism on the part of many.

Surely, there is a Godly in-between position requiring genuine Holy Spirit-inspired feelings. Those Jewish people celebrated joyfully in their feasts. Holy hands were held up. There is a modern tendency in churches to place a lot of emphasis on worship. People, especially the older ones, who have worshipped more quietly for most of their lives, find it hard to adapt and go along with change. So long as the Word of God is still honoured and preached this new emergence of demonstrative worship is surely a welcome obedience to Biblical teaching and it brings in the role of women as authentic priests. In God's estimate all believers are kings and priests to God offering the sacrifice of the fruit of their lips, which is their grateful praises. There will be differences of view about the number of decibels, how repetitive praises should be, and what instruments should be played. This does not negate the lessons that can be drawn from the meetings of the "common people" in the Court of the Tabernacle. The children of Israel sometimes worshipped God on the loud cymbals. I will express an interesting view about this class of Israelite in the following chapter.

Chapter Nine

OUT OF THE SHADOWS

> "The law is only a shadow of the good things that are coming – not the realities themselves." Hebrews 10.1

Inter-relationships

In the previous chapter I dealt in detail with the feasts of Israel and showed how these not only coincided remarkably on the Jewish sacred calendar with Christian holy days but also how these also possessed conjoined spiritual meanings. I was deliberately brief when it came to writing about the ordinances. I wanted to bring the old and new testaments startlingly into juxtaposition in one chapter so that this divine wonder has a common meeting place in the memory. The Bible has told us that things relating to ancient Israel have relevance for the present-day believer and, as you will see, this was not an understatement. It also reveals that all who have the faith of Abraham are members of the Israel of God. There is no such thing as Jew or Greek, male or female; all are one in Christ. This came about when the curtain in the Temple (the middle wall of partition) was ripped apart miraculously at the death of Jesus. The Old Covenant of the Law as handed down at Mount Sinai, or as it was amplified by Moses, did not explicitly discriminate against women but its ceremonies and feasts excluded their participation. The same was evident in the former practice of first sons serving in the tent of meeting. Was the preference for men due to custom in the first place or was it borne out of an innate male trait of dominance?

The Holy Place

As far as ordinances were concerned, the most appropriate item to consider first is the Holy Place because it stood in an intermediate position between the Holiest of All and the Court of the Tabernacle. It also speaks of service. Here stood the table with the shewbread, the golden lamps and the golden altar. The table and the shewbread, unknowingly to Israel, represented the Lord Jesus as the bread of life. The light from the oil filled candlesticks shone on the shewbread and represented the work of the Holy Spirit who glorifies Christ, and not Himself. Another instruction, and relevant to my main argument about the role of women, is that the congregation were to bring in beaten oil to fuel the lampstand. Intercession, worship and praise by the priests was part of the order of service. This oil-bringing should now have its counterpart in Christianity. When Paul described the manner of worship in the early Church it was apparent that the people came as spirit-filled vessels, or living stones, and then, collectively, comprised a habitation of praise and worship. By then the "common people" were all kings and priests to God and that meant men and women. The lamps in the tabernacle were to be kept burning from evening to morning and this can be taken to point towards the true Church whose light is to shine throughout the night of Christ's rejection by the world. There can be no doubt that, as reported of the Corinthian Church, when believers came together both men and women participated. One had a psalm to sing, one had some doctrine to impart, or a revelation to give, or was ready to speak in unknown tongues, or to interpret it.

I was discussing the exclusion of women by some Christian organisations this afternoon with a fellow Gideon. He expressed a view that churches were falling behind twenty-first-century society as far as the recognition of women is concerned. Although I shared his disappointment I felt that the last thing the Church should do was to follow secular trends per se. The real case, surely, was that it needed to get back to apostolic days. How Paul upbraided some in Galatia, wondering what had bewitched them! These had returned to the weak and beggarly elements of the law after having been set at liberty by the truth that was in Jesus Christ. Paul by his combined extraordinary knowledge of Judaism, and later his gift of knowledge, was able to relate the Jewish ordinances to God's great new pattern of worship. So much so as far as earthly service and worship was concerned.

The Holiest of All

Herein was the Ark of the Covenant in which were the Tablets of the Law, the Golden Pot of Manna and Aaron's rod that blossomed. Then there was the Mercy Seat and Cherubim. This was the place of reconciliation into which the High Priest entered once a year to make atonement for his own sins and the sins of the people. The blood of bulls and of goats (this was not effectual) was sprinkled on the Mercy Seat. This was a sacred sanctuary that was a go-between of heaven and earth. The glory of God came down and justice and mercy met. The reason that the Holy of Holies could only be entered once a year, and then by one man, was that this was only a concession. The Holy Spirit was signifying that the way in was not yet manifest. This earthly tabernacle would at some point have to be done away with. It was only a figure for the time being. The Mercy Seat speaks of the atonement of Christ and his propitiation and intercessory ministry. He is now the minister of the true tabernacle in the heavens which God pitched and not man. That tabernacle is his person. A tabernacle not made with hands. The Bible states of the ark in the wilderness: "That Ark which followed them was Christ."

The writer to the Hebrews reasoned that if the Jewish ordinances were acceptable to God as an interim measure, how much more does the blood of Christ, who through the eternal spirit offered himself without spot, purge our consciences from dead works to serve a living God. In the heavenly sanctuary, Jesus a high priest of the Order of Melchisedec, is the mediator of the new and eternal covenant.

Christ has entered the heavenly veil by the blood he shed. Sin's own debt is cancelled. This is a more excellent ministry. The Holy Spirit testified that God would put His laws into people's hearts and minds, and that their sins would be remembered no more. From henceforth an individual could enter into the holiest by the blood of Jesus. This was by a new and living way which Jesus had consecrated for them, through the veil. They could draw near with a full assurance of faith. I will enlarge on a definition of the people under the Court of the Tabernacle.

The Court of the Tabernacle

This was a very large rectangular area closed off with curtains. Its other features were a Gate of the Court, a Brazen Laver and a Brazen Altar.

As a reminder, the totality of people involved in overall worship comprised: the High Priest; the Aaronic Priests; the ordinary Levites, and The Common People. Collectively these were the Israelites, chosen of God. I have described how the priests were occupied in the Holy of Holies and the Holy Place, and will now turn my attention to usage of the Court of the Tabernacle. The ordinary Levites erected, transported and maintained all the physical components.

The court was a place of preparation. Without ceremonial washing and sacrifice the priests could not enter the tabernacle itself. This is why the Brazen Laver and the Brazen Altar were in the Court. Interestingly, the common people were permitted access through its gate. In fact there was only one entrance for all whether High Priest, priest, the Common People. There is now only one High Priest, Jesus, who made one sacrifice for sin and then sat down at the right hand of the Father on high. I will show that an authentic Christian in our new and better covenant is both a priest and one of the "Common People" as well. In that we serve and worship the Lord we are kings and priests to God. In that we are born anew, we are one of a ransomed throng. There are no longer classes of Christian, only those with different gifts and callings. There is no differentiation between men and women.

Transition

The Mosaic Law had to suffice until something better emerged on the road to full redemption. The second covenant was a better covenant because it was established on better promises. God found fault with the first covenant. Indeed if it had been perfect there would have been no point in finding a place for a second one. The law was weak, not that it was necessarily bad but that it could merely accuse. Paul said that the commandment came and he was aware of sin. The Bible says that if there had been a law that could bring righteousness there would have been such a law. The Levite priesthood was imperfect because its High Priest was made after the law of a carnal commandment.

The first covenant which God made when he took the children of Israel out of Egypt was broken because they did not continue in it. It was ready to wax away, and it did. Jesus would become the Great High Priest in the heavens where He would be the minister of the true and heavenly tabernacle not pitched by man but by God. He could not be a high priest on earth because he was of the tribe of Judah (a kingly line) and not a Levite.

The True Tabernacle

Of course the Mosaic tabernacle had features that corresponded to the "True Tabernacle". The Aaronic priesthood and the ceremonial on the Day of Atonement enabled the people to bring their offerings to God continually. It is wonderful that Jesus offered Himself on earth (as figuratively on the altar of the outer Court or Temple – he actually suffered "without the gate") and by his blood purged the heavenly things and places and sat down on the throne of glory in the heavenly Holy of Holies. There needs to be no more sacrifice for sin but the work of Jesus as a mediator began and continues. For both of these reasons there was, obviously, no more need for Aaronic priests to function on earth. The writer to the Hebrews told them that the introduction of a new covenant made the first one old.

Shadow of good things

Only in Christ was forgiveness and salvation to be found because the law was completely powerless to bring these about. It only provided people with a shadowy outline of the good things that were to come: atonement and sanctification. In burnt offerings and sacrifices for sin God had no pleasure. These Aaronic priests stood daily, ministering and offering the same sacrifices which were ineffectual. Jesus Christ offered one sacrifice for sins forever! All people could henceforth enter into the heavenly Holy of Holies by the blood of Jesus which was a new and living way consecrated for us through the veil of His flesh. Because there was now a high priest over the house of God, people could draw near with a full assurance of faith having their hearts sprinkled from an evil conscience and their bodies washed with pure water.

Non sequitur (a false conclusion)

I seek to understand others who have different opinions from my own. I also give credit to them whenever it is deserved. I am going to take the case of a theological scholar who lived over 150 years ago. He was a canon in the Church of England. His expositions blessed many. However, he had a problem. He had to justify his position as a minister and also the then exclusion of women from ordination. He did not dissent from most of the Biblical teaching from Hebrews that I have been providing in this chapter. So how did he argue? He quoted no New Testament scriptures. He drew firstly on the Old Testament teaching of the Aaronic priesthood that is obsolete and, secondly, upon the Early Fathers whom I would not touch, in this respect, with a barge pole! He avoided referring to Hebrews, particularly in respect of the abolition of the law.

Of all places he went to the first epistle of Peter, Chapter 2. This is the very place in which the Great Apostle concludes that in the new creation all people (men and women) are as living stones, a holy priesthood, to offer up spiritual sacrifices, acceptable to God by Christ Jesus. These are the very scriptures that bring women into freedom. Quoting Augustine, this canon says that Christians are in fact one priesthood, collectively, and individually only in a limited, but definite sense. But, he says, this does not trench upon the peculiar province of our one High Priest (fine so far) nor on the other hand does it exclude the office of a vicarious priesthood, representing and acting on behalf of the body corporate (O dear!). This, he goes on, is sufficiently proven from passages in the Old Testament, which at once recognise the people as priests (not really – only some Levites), yet restrict certain functions to the Aaronic priesthood (I thought this was proven to be obsolete). He, again, cites Augustine and then Irenaeus, and goes on – by parity of reasoning all ministers and stewards of the mysteries of Christ constitute a true, though vicarious and representative priesthood. He quotes Waterland's *Distinctions of Sacrifice.* I find the whole argument totally unconvincing. There is no more need of sacrifice other than praises, which are the fruit of the lips, from all Christians. It would seem that this man, like the great Martin Luther, was free on the grounds of justification by faith yet still bound by the religiosity of a sacramental system, albeit in Luther's case a modified consubstantiation.

Throw out the bondwomen

Paul was perplexed that the Galatians wanted to go back under the law. Had they actually read it, and particularly about Abraham's two sons? One was born of a bondwoman, Hagar, and the other of a freewomen, Sarah. The first was born in the course of nature (Ishmael) and the other (Isaac) by the power of God's promise. All that is an allegory, the two women stand for the two dispensations. Hagar stands for the old dispensation, which brings up children to bondage, the dispensation which comes to us from Mount Sinai. Mount Sinai in Arabia, has the same meaning in the allegory as Jerusalem, the Jerusalem which exists here and now; an enslaved city whose children are slaves. Whereas our mother is the heavenly Jerusalem (the city Abraham sought) – a city of freedom. Believers are the children of promise as Isaac was. Now, as then, the son who was born in the course of nature persecutes the son whose birth is a spiritual birth. But what does the scripture say? Rid yourself of the bondwoman and her son; it cannot be that the son of the bondwoman should divide the inheritance with the son of a freewoman.

Freedom for all

Because of His great love for us, God who is rich in mercy made us alive in Christ even when we were dead in transgressions – it is by grace you have been saved. And God raised us up with Him in the heavenly realms in Christ Jesus. Our life is hid with Christ in God. Now in all of this, are we just talking about men? Since all believers are free from the law and the traditions of men under which they are ordered to touch not, taste not, handle not, or to observe days and moons, the functionaries of all these things are redundant. Attempts to perpetuate religious man-made rules and regulations are merely instruments of domination. Introductions of practices, for instance, the auricular confession of sins to men, are, surely, unseemly. It is unwholesome to require a woman to confess her sins to a celibate man. There is no room in a new creation for leaders to exercise lordship over people like the kings of the gentiles do. He that would be greatest must be the servant of all. God sets in the church apostles, evangelists, pastors and teachers but this is for the perfection of believers, for building them up and to prepare them for works of service: not just to impress them with pomp and elaborate ritual.

There is no contradiction in John's epistles where he says on the one hand that those who say they are without sin are liars, and on the other that that those who are born of God do not sin. John was writing in the first instance of the sinful nature inherited by all from Adam, and in the second to the divine nature bestowed at conversion. Christ's humanity was sinless because He was not born of the will of man but of God. A believer has both a sinful Adamic nature and is also a partaker of the divine nature that was in Christ. These two natures are contrary one to the other and conflict. The believer is to have no confidence in the former and reckon it dead on a daily basis. Paul described how he found himself not being able to do the things he wanted to, and, instead, doing the things he did not want to do. He wrote: "O wretched man that I am. Who can free me from the body of this death?" He found that by the Spirit of Christ he could do all things through Christ who strengthened him. He got the victory.

Sanctification

This is a subject that normally I steer away from for two reasons. Firstly, it smacks of presumption to talk of being sanctified, and secondly because there is an error going abroad that one can attain to sinless perfection in this life. Even John and Charles Wesley dabbled with such a doctrine. My earlier comments about the old and new natures put things into more balance. It is only that which is born of God that does not sin. It is not possible to improve the new nature, and for that matter it is not possible to improve the sinful nature; that is why it must be reckoned as dead each day. Therefore, in a de jure sense sanctification is purchased by Christ. However, de facto, it is a matter of progression.

Once again, allow me to refer to the Law. Even to this day when Moses is read the veil is upon the hearts of those who are still under it. However, when people turn to the Lord the veil is taken away. Where the Spirit of the Lord is there is liberty. Note that this means liberty for everyone. We all, with open face beholding as in a glass the glory of the Lord, are changed into the same image from glory to glory as by the Spirit of the Lord. We all become more fitted for service in a kingdom where the High Priest takes care of the spiritual Holy of Holies and men and women undertake all the earthly functions of service, worship and nurturing.

PART II

CUSTOM, CULTURE, AND TRADITION

Chapter Ten

WOMEN AND RELIGIOUS TRADITION

> "You nullify the word of God for the sake of your tradition."
> Matthew 15:6.

Testing tradition

Jesus had a quarrel with tradition and so do I. It is not that tradition is worthless: far from it. It is only in so far that it conflicts with the will of God that I fall out with it. Jesus saw that in a number of respects that the imposition of certain traditions had an effect of nullifying His word. I am concerned here to show how tradition has resulted in the subjugation of women in most unfair ways.

The priesthood

I am not intent upon being critical of the views of others. I am, rather, trying to confine opposition to those views that deny women a fuller spiritual role. Orthodoxy, in a broad sense, gives equal weight to the Bible and tradition. Although I seek to respect traditionalists and try to understand their reasoning, I cannot, myself, agree with any tradition that flies in the face of Biblical truth or that any of it is equal to the Bible.

Since there is no New Testament justification for earthly sacrificing priests because the Old Testament Aaronic Priesthood has been abolished, the justification for a continuing sacrificing priesthood must rest upon tradition. The Roman Catholic catechism does pull a scripture out of the Old Testament to justify sacrifice: "From the rising of the sun to the going down thereof my name shall be great amongst the Gentiles ("heathen?" AV), and in every place there will be a sacrifice (AV rendering is that incense shall be offered in my name) and there shall be offered in my name a clean oblation." (Malachi: 1.11) However, a clean oblation would refer to the offering of bread and wine in the manner of Melchisedec, and incense is a type of prayer and praise being offered up rather than a physical sacrifice. Of the latter there is no longer any need. It is significant that women are debarred from this kind of priesthood.

It is possible for sake of argument for orthodox theologians to descend into sheer sophistry. For example the notes in The Jerusalem Bible seek to diminish the standing of a simple breaking of bread service and to replace this with a concept of a priestly Eucharist. (Note: the Jerusalem Bible translation is a thundering good one. I am only referring to its notes that are a present-day opinion.) Paul writes in 1 Corinthians about decorum in public worship, and deplores misbehaviour in the breaking of bread. When the early Christians met from house to house they obeyed the injunction of the Lord to remember his death as often as they gathered together. However some were getting drunk and some were bringing their own supper and gobbling it up even before others arrived. It is abundantly clear, even to my simple mind, that Paul was condemning bad behaviour and not the practice laid down by the Lord Himself. Now it was not until hundreds of years later that men coined the word "Eucharist" and brought in an idea that it was a sacrifice of the new law called "the Mass". In order to bring into disrepute the simple breaking of bread service followed by early Christians and many Christians today, this Bible footnote takes up Paul's comment with the following note, "the point is, when you hold these meetings it is not the Lord's Supper." It is clear that Paul was referring to drunkenness and gluttony and not to a Bible-based breaking of bread and that to present bad behaviour as a proof of spiritual invalidity was a specious argument.

A present-day sacrificing priesthood and a doctrine of a Eucharist rests firmly on tradition and this status quo is a sincere and key element of orthodoxy. I am concerned here that this is a system that weighs against the rights of women. It is a complex issue because I have already argued that there should not be sacrificing women priests on the ground that the whole priesthood function is obsolete, except in so far as it is uniquely bound up eternally with our one great High Priest Jesus Christ. But please refer to my placatory comments in the Introduction. I am persisting in my argument because if the tradition was swept away and the Church reverted to a really apostolic agenda there would no longer be any need to exclude women.

The Virgin Mary

We should be very grateful to orthodoxy for championing the doctrine of the Virgin Birth. It is a critical doctrine that underpins the deity of Christ and of his sinless birth as the first born of a new creation. I was speaking only last week with a senior academic at a degree ceremony. He had recently converted to Rome from Anglicanism on the grounds that he had become disenchanted with the nothingness of liberals. They did not believe in such fundamental things as the Virgin Birth and a literal Resurrection. He felt that Catholics were much more positive than this, and he was right.

Mary was the most wonderful handmaid of the Lord and all nations have called her blessed. It seems to me that tradition suffered from an absentia complex at one stage. As the memory of the historic Jesus faded some really saintly contemporary people drew admiration. When these died, they were revered, perhaps excessively, and so the practice of canonising saints and praying to them sprang up. Initially, Mary was regarded as an historic reality. Thomas Aquinas taught against a new idea that Mary was born sinless (as is taught today) by pointing out that she rejoiced in Christ her Saviour. His teaching was simply put on the back burner when Bernadette Siborous had a vision of Mary declaring herself to be the Immaculate Conception. So again beliefs were introduced that were extra-Biblical. Another point I wish to make is that this vision was the experience of a woman who gained considerable respect. It did not add to the status of mortal woman. Bernadette spent the rest of her life cloistered in a convent.

The doctrine of the Assumption of Mary into heaven is based on tradition as is her assumed role as Queen of Heaven. Understandable Protestant objections to Marian doctrines such as this have, unintentionally, detracted from Mary's rightful status in the eyes of many. I must allow that there is a strong probability that Mary is highly regarded in heaven on the basis of reward, as opposed to salvific merit. But who am I, or anybody else, to conjecture about heavenly things? This tradition is all very well but it rests upon conjecture and other-worldliness. Its introduction has not improved the position of women one iota. Even the worship (dulia) given to Mary by Roman Catholic theologians and

Vatican II's reference to Mary as a "Mediatrix" has not bestowed any more earthly merit on other living members of her sex.

Celibacy

Both Jesus and the Apostle Paul spoke about celibacy. Jesus Himself was celibate and so was Paul at the time of his Christian ministry. He was probably married at some earlier stage because as a member of the Sanhedrin marriage would have been a requirement. As recorded in the nineteenth chapter of Matthew's Gospel, Jesus made it clear that celibacy was not for everyone. People could be born with celibate inclinations; they could be celibate through subsequent physical circumstances, or they could receive a calling to be celibate for the sake of the kingdom. In the latter instance a person had to be capable of accepting such a style of life. It should be personally accepted and not an imposed condition. Paul gave identical instruction. He wrote to the Corinthians that every man had his proper gift from God. Importantly he made two points. Firstly those who did not have the gift of celibacy were better off if they married. Secondly, he wrote to Timothy that it was wrong to forbid people to marry or to command them to abstain from meats.

Enforced celibacy on either sex is detrimental to the happiness of the individual if they do not have a special calling. In the beginning man and woman were essentially companions. After the fall they were told by God to increase and multiply. These are two sound reasons for Jesus and Paul seeing marriage as the norm and celibacy as the exception. Tradition has placed compulsory celibacy upon priests and nuns with devastating results. Enforced priestly celibacy is thought to rest on a plan to introduce a superior class of Christian and also a need to keep confessors safe from any possible form of betrayal of secrets. Compulsory celibacy has resulted latterly in significant numbers of clergy becoming paedophiles. There seems little justification for enforced celibacy and its unfortunate effect of excluding suitable women from sharing pastoral work with a husband.

It is premature to speculate too much about the affect paedophilia will have on Rome's future attitude to celibacy of priests. Reported rumblings in the Curia are of possible relaxation of the present prohibition. Scripture does not require compulsory abstinence from marrying. An early reply to these rumblings is a claim that priests receive a spiritual gift to remain unmarried. This simply mirrors the age-old ecclesiastical fiction that spiritual things can be appropriated with a rubber stamp.

Traditions of men

Jesus knew what was in men. He quickly distinguished between true faith and professing religion. He upbraided the Pharisees for teaching the doctrines of men. They erred because they did not know the scriptures. They made clean the outside of the cup whereas inside they were as ravening wolves. That is rather hard stuff! They were allowed to have more than one wife, "because of their hardness of heart". They thought so little of their wives that Jesus was able to crack a joke. It was a most ridiculous reason to give for not attending a marriage to say one had married a wife. Today women are prevented from becoming bishops (who anoint people in the ceremony of Confirmation) despite the fact that the Son of God was content that women should anoint his feet.

Jesus condemned the Scribes and the Pharisees for paying tithes in mint and cumin, but omitted weightier matters such as judgment, and mercy, and faith. They strained at a gnat and swallowed a camel. My father was bound by a tradition that he must fast from midnight if he was going to receive communion. My mother usually made preparations for the Sunday lunch in advance and had shelled some peas and put these in a colander. As my father was going out he inadvertently ate a single pea. A priest would not allow him to receive communion. It was the same sort of mindset that was in denial for years about problems of child abuse. Most Catholics abhorred the state of affairs as much as anybody else. It was a catastrophe that impacted on Catholic mothers most. Some one might wonder if this state of affairs would have existed in a like degree if there had been women priests, or at the least male priests had an option of marrying. This is hypothetical, so it is better to stay with my main point which is that all unregenerate people are more susceptible to evil and temptation than are regenerate believers. This leaves their sex out of the equation.

Weaker ground

Although orthodoxy insists that tradition is equal to scripture, I challenge such an assertion. Tradition is what men choose to make of it. It is more difficult to overturn scripture even when it has been mishandled. Take for instance the unfortunate tradition of Limbo. This is supposedly a more pleasant part of Hades to which deceased infants who have not been baptised are said to be consigned because they are not considered to be in a fit state to see God. I know of a couple who had an infant who died at birth. A vicar told them to put the body in a box and bury it somewhere as it could not be buried in consecrated ground. I was able to give them a much better picture of the nature of God. The Roman Catholic Church has abandoned this doctrine of Limbo by stealth. It dropped it out of its latest catechism and substituted a teaching that Jesus said, "suffer the little children to come to me". This is real progress made more possible because the doctrine of Limbo is based on Greek tradition and not the Bible. Could it be that, gradually, orthodoxy will loosen its grip of male domination on account of such authority resting more on tradition than on scripture? I am alleging that, despite orthodox claims of the equality of Biblical and traditional teaching, tradition is founded on weaker ground.

Papal infallibility

There is hope that the doctrine of papal infallibility will eventually be revoked. It was introduced by a Pope in office in the latter part of the nineteenth century. It is not half as difficult to abandon as many suppose. It does not mean that he cannot make a mistake as a man. It is only when he defines a doctrine concerning faith or morals and writes *ex cathedra* to the whole Church it is said that he cannot be wrong. To understand the motive, if not the manner in which the teaching was presented, one has to see that the Pope was to be the arbiter of what the Church should believe. It was a discipline that was intended to prevent schism and fragmentation such as seen in nonconformity. Unfortunately, with an iron fist, any dissenter was excommunicated. Hans Kung, a distinguished German Catholic theologian, had his teaching licence withdrawn for challenging papal infallibility. If one day a future humble Pope acknowledges that he is only the Bishop of Rome and delegates authority to a College of Cardinals it would facilitate the possibility of change. There would be an avenue in which to review women's rights without the embarrassment of challenging former infallibility.

Traditions are being eroded in orthodoxy. People can go to obligatory Mass on Saturday evening when previously it was a mortal sin not to go without excuse on a Sunday. It is no longer obligatory to abstain from meat or soups made from meat on Fridays. Women no longer have to wear hats in church. Communion can be taken by hand rather than on the tongue. Deacons can conduct marriages and perform other duties hitherto the reserve of priests. Irish priests can now go to the races in Ireland instead of packing out ferries to Liverpool on race days.

Growth of tradition

It is necessary to look at length as to how tradition grew and to ponder about the way the freedom of women in the early Church was gradually eroded by its advance. Its progress was not without opposition and it is not realised by many that Christian tradition has been steadily added to over two millennia. A common definition of tradition is that it is the handing down of information by word of mouth from generation to generation. Jesus had a problem with Jewish tradition. He said on one occasion to Jewish leaders that they nicely set aside the commandments of God in order to keep their tradition. He also quoted a prophecy of Isaiah who said, "This people honours me with their lips, but their heart is far away from me, but in vain do they worship me, teaching as their doctrine the commandments of men."

I have been critical of how early Church fathers handled the word of God. However, some of them uttered dire warnings about the dangers of introducing tradition into divine affairs. Tertullian wrote, "I do not receive what you bring of your own without the scripture… . It is not lawful for us to indulge unto our own choice or to choose what anyone brings in of his own choosing. We have the good example set by the Apostles who brought in nothing of their own minds. Having received teaching from Jesus they communicated it sublimely to the nations." Jerome wrote, "That which hath not authority from the scripture is as easily despised as it is asserted. But those other things which, without authority or testimony of scripture they find out or feign of their own accord as of apostolic tradition, the sword of God smites through". Basil wrote, "It hast the manifest guilt of infidelity and pride to reject anything that is written or to add or to introduce anything that is not written." Chrysostom wrote, "Who is it that promises these things? Paul. For we are not to say anything without testimony, nor upon our mere reasoning: for if anything be spoken without scripture the mind of the heavens fluctuates, now assenting, anon hesitating, sometimes rejecting what is spoken as frivolous, sometimes receiving it as probable. But where the testimony of the divine voice comes forth from scripture, it confirms the word of the speaker and mind of the hearer."

It needs to be realised that orthodoxy has been responsible for keeping women from participating in ministry partly by its continual addition to the deposit of faith found in the Bible. Its actions have distorted the purity of the faith once delivered to the saints (saved ones). Tradition was particularly recognised by The Council of Trent (1545-1563). This, firstly, reserved the interpretation of scripture as the sole right of the Church, secondly decreed the divine authority of the apocryphal books, and, thirdly, opened up the way to the acceptance of tradition. It added that Catholic tradition can be said to consist of all those truths which, though not committed to writing, under divine inspiration, have been handed down within the Church from age to age in various ways; many of them are found in the works of the Fathers of the Church, many in the teachings of the Popes and Councils; and many are drawn from early paintings and inscriptions found in the catacombs.

It is not the purpose of this book to go in any detail into ritual and objects used in orthodoxy that are not supportable from scripture. These only impinge subordinately upon the religious freedom of women. As examples, however, the following are noted: holy oils, holy candles, incense, blessed ashes, the crucifix, and an earthly tabernacle. Then there are relics, vestments, and the Roman missal. However, an appendix provides a calendar of additions over a whole millennium. (See Appendix 2.)

The suggestion that tradition always existed, was later revealed, and then introduced into written canon law is not sustainable. There have always been factions within the Church and when one triumphs its doctrines become the order. An example is the triumph of the Ultramontanes over the Gallicans. This led to the doctrines of Papal Infallibility and the Immaculate Conception and the worship of the human hearts of Jesus and Mary. These additions were made in the late nineteenth century, were influenced by the teachings of Alphonsus Ligouri and certainly not a part of previous Catholic thinking. The false decretals and the Clementine literature were produced to bolster up the concept of Roman Catholic supremacy.

Tradition's bed fellows

I will be writing in the following chapters about other factors that have weighed adversely against the chances of women being counted as equal to men in the Lord's service. They have been oppressed by a combination of tradition, culture and custom. In some instances the reasons have been circumstantial, and in others it has been due to the hardness of the hearts of men. Man has tribal instincts, now manifested in more civilised society in the guise of nationalism, and in the Church by entrenched denominationalism. Both are extremely deleterious and it is hoped that moderation will permit greater personal liberty, especially that of women.

Apologia

Although strictures have been placed upon tradition and it is contended these are merited in relation to attitudes towards women, this is not a complete story. Faults lie primarily with power-seeking leaderships. There is a rump of ordinary people in every walk of life who despite allegiances do all manner of good. This is attested to by Baroness Caroline Cox, a great Christian Anglican, who is the inspiration behind HART (a humanitarian charity). She has personally endured dangers in frequent visits to such troubled areas of the world as Armenia, Nigeria, Sudan, Darfur, Uganda, Burma, and Indonesia. Both those who suffer torture, death and persecution and those who bravely go to their rescue are of every background. Therefore, a case of being "in Christ" must be tempered by an acknowledgment that God is all-loving. Yes, the gospel cannot be compromised. However it is not within my province to fathom all of God's ways or to predict what his final attitude towards the nations will be. There is no case for being judgmental towards the "rump" referred to. Whether this relates to religious traditionalists, humanists, or atheists, or those of other faiths there is ample evidence of kindness towards fellow mortals. The extreme Calvinistic doctrine of the total depravity of all but "the elect" is unsustainable in the light of history. Mankind has great secular institutions governing social provision. It is just that these are imperfect and short of divine standards.

Chapter Eleven

WOMEN AND DENOMINATIONALISM

> Are you not acting like mere men? For one says, "I follow Paul," and another says, "I follow Apollos": are you not mere men?

Dependence of sheep

Most ordinary Church members have a limited understanding of the detailed tenets of their denomination. This is not surprising because they have livings to earn and families to bring up. Many are brought up in a faith and are loyal to their parents' tradition so it is not surprising if they rely upon clergy for instruction, and why not if this proves to be sound? The trouble is that they are often given particular brands of Biblical interpretation. Generally, in founding a new denomination its leaders did not advance the case of women. I am reluctant to concentrate upon the weakness of any one denomination in this respect because the phenomenon was endemic. I have, therefore, picked an unlikely one in which autocratic behaviour is more subtle.

An example

I am only singling out this denomination as an example to show that even in relatively moderate cases the across-the-board inclinations of men still come to the fore. Their innate tendency to suppose women are inferior to themselves is ever-present. Within most creeds and confessions there lurk unwritten assumptions that men must be in the driving seat. I have selected the great family of Presbyterian churches as my example, only exposing its imperfections when these directly or indirectly impinge on my subject of women's rights. Women have not been treated in accordance with scripture in most of these churches. One is not dealing here with papal infallibility, but with something more subtle. Ostensibly, nonconformity brought believers into greater liberty, but in reality this is only what they are led to believe.

In passing, I note that the origin of the Westminster Confession, which is the basis of Presbyterianism, was a corollary of the Canons of Dort, (this was a result of a hurriedly convened civic government committee!). The canons also align with the Thirty Nine Articles of the Church of England. The findings were influenced by the teachings of John Calvin and Martin Luther. Such teachings relied heavily upon scripture, or rather their interpretation of scripture. I have no gripe about this, believing that people have a right to their own opinions. I like Voltaire's famous quotation that he would die to preserve a person's right to an opinion even if he did not agree with it. There is the difference. People are bound today by what is laid down for them in catechisms and confessions. In reality they have not as much freedom of conscience as is supposed.

Disappointment

Let me tell you about the "sell". The Westminster Confession was substantially the work of seven men of their day. It triumphantly proclaimed that: "God alone is Lord of the human conscience, which is responsible only to His authority. God has set the human conscience free from all obligations to believe or obey any such doctrines or commandments of men as are either contrary to or aside from the teachings of His word. And because the powers which God hath ordained, and the liberty which Christ hath purchased are not intended by God to destroy, but mutually to uphold and preserve one another; they who upon pretence of Christian liberty shall oppose any lawful power, or the lawful exercise of it, whether it be civil or *ecclesiastical,* resist the ordinance of God." Then regard the twist! "This Christian liberty is not, however, absolute. It has its distinct end and limits. The limits of this liberty are of two kinds: (a) Authority of God, the Lord of conscience. (b) The equal liberties and rights of our fellow-men, with whom we dwell in organised societies. (As an aside, it has not worked out to mean *fellow-women* as well.) It continues – "to claim that as God has established the Church, obedience to it is an essential part of obedience to God. The Church has a right from God of exercising its discipline upon any who maintain or practise opinions or actions plainly contrary to the doctrines of Scripture". Of course this means seven men's interpretations of it! They became "the Church".

Thanks to Abraham Lincoln

The sum of all this is that instead of possessing actual personal liberty of conscience, people were bound by the opinions of seven ordinary men of their day. They disagreed at their peril. An inner cognoscenti was arrogating power to itself. Thankfully, the freedom granted at the present day by Western democracies has pulled the teeth of little religious tyrants. No longer can the religious leaders connive to have dissenters put to death. Both Calvin and Arminius were self-opinionated men. It is not surprising, although the Pilgrim Fathers fled to America to enjoy religious freedom, that in a very short space of time they were putting to death, in Massachusetts, feeble-minded women on the grounds that they were witches. There is no record of men being executed as wizards!

We are "the mob"

So arrogant were the seven men that on the one hand they window-dressed their views and on the other discreetly proclaimed that all ecclesiastical power was vested in the Church, none of its members excluded, and then went on to describe those members as a mob. Power was vested in ministers as the highest class of officers. How many Presbyterians know that they are regarded as a mob? Or how many know that they are as much under their overseer's thumbs as Catholics are of an imposed priesthood?

A miscellany

More enlightened denominations admit women into the ministry on an equal basis with men. I have mentioned some. The Salvation Army, most Pentecostal movements, and Methodist churches have enlightened agendas about the freedom of women. Those denominations that allow local independence, as opposed to operating central control, vary according to majority views. Baptist churches were originally the province of men and so the introduction of women into ministry has been gradual. When some of these churches appoint women as Pastors, even in lay roles, it is at the risk of losing dissenting members by transfer to more conservative churches.

Evangelical churches are more rigid except in cases where new churches are set up independently without recourse to the Fellowship of Independent Evangelical Churches. I will be referring to the hiatus in the Church of England more fully in a later chapter. Because it is a broad church it has been possible to introduce women clergy but not women bishops. This church is divided on the issue of woman's ministry and is facing the likelihood of disaffection or even a complete split.

A rich and influential woman

The Countess of Huntingdon had a big impact across a doctrinal divide. She supported the Wesley brothers, John and Charles, George Whitefield, and the saintly John Fletcher of Madeley. Since she was engaging with men who were Calvinistic, Arminian, and Anglican, and getting them to meet amicably at Trefecca, achieving harmony was no mean feat. And this was in days when assessments of others' religious views were usually spelled out in vitriolic language. The Countess's close friend Mrs Mary Delany was able to associate intellectually with men of diverse denominational backgrounds such as her second husband Dean Patrick Delany DD, Jonathan Swift, George Frederick Handel, Captain Cook, King George III, and the Duke of Wellington when a boy. She was a patron of St James's Church in Piccadilly, and according to a recent biography written by Roy Hattersley, when she was the widowed Mrs Mary Purves, became a girl friend of John Wesley. She was a woman of great faith and generous disposition. There are ten published biographies of her life recording her invention of paper collage, shell design, her herbarium of Captain Cook's specimens of the South Seas, her court dress designs now in the British Museum, her famous diaries, and her close association with the royal family. In her widowhood she lived in a grace-and-favour house in the grounds of Windsor Castle. Today her portrait hangs in the castle itself. There is a monument to her in St James' Church. The most important thing about her life to us is that she maintained a strong Christian witness and was a link between the English and Irish Churches. She encouraged Handel in his faith (he was her next-door neighbor for a time in Brook Street, Mayfair), and as she was no mean organist it is not surprising *The Messiah* was performed for the first time in Dublin in deference to her. This was in the presence of her husband and Jonathan Swift.

Neither of these two ladies had any prospect of being used in direct ministry even though the Countess founded a whole string of churches. There were two of these until quite recently in the area of Brentwood in Essex, and I preached in both quite regularly.

Queens of England

The Synod of the Church of England has not quite got around to approving the appointment of women as bishops. Yet queens of England can be constitutional heads of that church. Queens Elizabeth I, Queen Anne, Queen Victoria, and our present beloved Elizabeth II have all filled this role. Queen Mary Tudor did not fill it as she followed the Roman Catholic tradition. Our Queen Elizabeth has been a great example of the effectiveness of women of faith. Exempt from political correctness, her vibrant Christmas messages of the Christ child are heard by millions of people around the world. What earns her the greatest respect is that her words are matched with a character that is constant, dutiful, and a credit to her country. Queen Alexandra was not a constitutional monarch but the extent of her giving to Christian social causes was a slight embarrassment to the royal budget.

Nuns

An arm of service open to women in orthodoxy is that of joining an order of nuns. Duties can vary from purely spiritual functions like praying, liturgical, and sacristan, to teaching, hospital and hospice, and social work. There are lower orders who engage in menial duties such as looking after the needs of higher orders, cleaning, washing, and laundry duties. At one time these latter women were the ugly and least clever daughters of working-class families. Convent secondary schools are today among the best in the country. People send their daughters to these schools purely on their educational merit regardless of religious persuasion.

The work of Mother Theresa in Calcutta is a pointer to the effectiveness of women in missionary work. She drew worldwide admiration. Her theology, as a woman of humble origin was iconic, and consequently she had a faith crisis towards the end of her life. One can sympathise over her limited aspirations as a woman in orthodoxy. She will get more recognition in death as to status than she was entitled to in life, and will, no doubt, be canonised in due course by her church.

The Vatican has just launched an enquiry about the diverse services being offered by some orders of American nuns. Nuns are forsaking their traditional roles and reaching out in many ways to the community. They are abandoning religious dress. One order has started a work at San Pedro Hospital involved in the rehabilitation of male drug addicts. The Vatican is seeking to re-impose old disciplines. Some nuns of the Sacred Heart have left the Roman rite. The nuns think that the Vatican is too distant to be in touch with changes in American culture.

Hardliners

Just as there are enlightened men in the Church who seek to further the cause of women, so there are hard-liners who are more extreme than the confessions they subscribe to. I submitted a manuscript to a publisher once and it was sent to a reviewer. He telephoned me to say that he would recommend that it should go into the fast lane and that I would receive a contract within a week. Unfortunately, he had only read half of my script. When he found that the rest of it was too alive he pulled the whole work to pieces. I had expressed a view that it was wrong to label popes as "Anti-Christ". He wrote that, the great Protestant confessions describe the Pope as Anti-Christ because of the extravagant claims made by popes, and because he is head of a vast system which denies and contradicts the gospel. One of my views that got up his nose was that I had accorded a Roman Catholic woman the status of martyr. Elizabeth of York was tortured to make her renounce a faith she had been brought up in. She had paving stones placed over her one by one. She refused to renounce her faith and was crushed to death. I was not concerned about what denomination she belonged to. The reviewer wrote, "Catholic martyrs were executed for political chicanery – Protestants for refusal to believe in the Mass. This is a very important distinction." He treated me like a nincompoop although academically I could eat him for breakfast. But what did the Great Westminster Confession actually state about popes. Just read this: "The authors of our Confession can hardly have intended to declare that each individual Pope is the personal Anti-Christ." That is precisely what I wrote. I had opined that the Borgia popes came close to the description but I wrote (and this is underlined in my recent *Finger of God)* that men like Pope Leo XIII and Pope John II, despite belonging to the papal system, were genuine men of God.

So women are not only up against a general prejudice of many organised denominations. They are vulnerable to the incipient sniping of male extremists.

The Catholic Church still appears to be insensitive to the marital problems of its adherents. I cite a case of a young lady whose husband ran off with a young girl after only just over a year of marriage. Years later she met a man who had been deserted by a domineering wife. This couple had to marry outside of the Church by means of a civil marriage. They have two children and the man became a convert to Roman Catholicism. This family attends their local church and is actively involved in it. However, this couple can never attend communion as long as they live. The children have made their first communions. Whatever must go through the children's minds when they realise their parents are barred?

President Barack Obama

In a recent interview conducted by Rev Rick Warren the President of the United States of America stated, "I think the country's greatest failure in my lifetime has been that we still don't abide by that basic precept in Matthew that whatever you do to the least of my brothers you do for me." Clearly, his reference to "brothers" was a generic term for mankind, and his added remarks made this apparent. He continued, "And that basic principle applies to poverty, racism, and sexism. It applies to not thinking about ladders of opportunity for people to get into the middle class. There is a pervasive sense that this country, as wealthy and powerful as we are, still does not spend enough time thinking about the least of these."

Our closest attention

So why don't we spend more time in the Church thinking about sexism and how it should be dealt with? As was his predecessor, President Obama is an outgoing born-again believer. His remarks can be taken to apply equally to the Church and to secular society. One reason is complacency and the absence of a strong lobby. That is one as strong as GAFCOM that opposes women ministers. Another reason, already touched upon, is the absence of reference to women's rights in all the major denominational Christian confessions. What is not written in these goes, as to future action, into default mode.

I am leaving judgment as to what influence custom and culture exert on women's rights, or lack of them to the next chapter. It will be sufficient for me here, in order to aid overall comprehension, to remind readers that essentially women's rights in the Church should be spiritually determined. It is through their equal inheritance in Christ with men, as new creatures, that they should enjoy parity. Culture and custom are negative elements that have affected women's lives adversely. In themselves these elements neither grant nor withhold authority in the Church, but if these continue to influence attitudes within it, God's perfect plan will not be followed. This plan should remain inviolable and irrevocable. On the other hand if secular attitudes improve, women in the Church might derive some benefit as a result of making comparisons. But this will still be a mere milestone on the road leading to complete conformity to the divine will.

Decentralised Churches

The early Church knew nothing of denominations although there were factions. The growth of formal Christianity resulted in the proverbial tree that grew so big that birds rested in its branches. Christ foresaw the dangers of bureaucracy and arrogations of power.

Chapter Twelve

WOMEN, CUSTOM AND CULTURE

"Here feel we but the penalty of Adam." Wm Shakespeare. From *As You Like It.*

A Link

In this chapter I am dealing with the lot of women according to custom and as a result looking at the cultural environments in which they have lived. I am doing this so that I can make comparisons with the way that women have been treated in the Christian Church. First of all, I am making an important interjection by stating that some Christian expositors of the Bible have caused confusion by failing to recognise the differences, in the Bible, between custom (usually referred to as tradition) and spiritual reality. Just because facts are given in the Bible they assume these must all relate to spiritual matters, not realising that at every period of time all mankind was heavily conditioned by the ruling customs and culture. I will be expanding on this all-important fact in Chapter Fifteen.

Society, religion, and Jesus

This is a sad chapter about poor attitudes towards women in society in the course of history. Attitudes of men towards women in religion have been different but not necessarily any more generous. Changes in such attitudes in religion and in society have not followed the same trends. However, God does not change and God is not synonymous with professing religion. Jesus wore a seamless robe which is a good exemplar of his character. He was pre-eminently concerned with the welfare of others, especially the underprivileged. He is the same, yesterday, today and forever. As a contrast I see society garbed, and for that matter mere religion as well, in Donegal tweed with its variegated patterns. Unfortunately, God's real attitude towards women does not enter into certain men's consideration; they substitute their own version of it. I am leaving it to the next chapter to discuss more fully the vexed question of the historical changes in the status of women in religion. The factors of change in society, which I am dealing with here, are driven by economic circumstances, tribalism, nationalism, education, innovation, environmental issues, idealism, genocides, and sexual competitiveness. These factors are only partly controllable by mankind. In many instances change has been due to man's decisions, both brilliantly innovative and unutterably irresponsible, but in other cases the world has suffered from the unbridled forces of nature. On the other hand religious reform is, notionally, in the gift of leaders, but their efforts in bringing about the spiritual liberation of women have been puny. Correct interpretation of God's will has been hampered by man's selfish, innate, thinking.

Old custom

The ethos of custom is changed by the habits and inclinations of particular generations. In terms of what is ideal custom is not necessarily progressive. This was brought home in the superlative prose of the Bard. An exiled duke in the Forest of Arden asked, "Hath not old custom made this life more sweet than that of painted pomp? Are not these woods more free from peril than the envious court? Here feel we but the penalty of Adam: the season's difference as the icy fang and churlish chiding of the winter wind, which when it bites and blows upon my body even till I shrink with cold, I smile and say, this is no flattery – these are counsellors that feelingly persuade me what I really am. Sweet are the uses of adversity, which like the toad ugly and venomous, wears yet a precious jewel upon its head; and this our life, exempt from public haunt, find tongues in trees, books in running brooks, sermons in stones, and good in everything. I would not change it."

Here was a man who had experienced the worldly, artificial luxury of the court and been captivated by it. Through circumstances beyond his control he was exiled into a forest. What made him adapt in such a way so as to help him to be more at peace in a primitive environment?

Was it the numinous in him? It was because God had set eternity in his heart!

It is alleged that people who speak of what they term, "The good old days", tend to forget things that were bad about them. There have been many times in history when custom was influenced by moral conviction and also by the lack of it. For example, Rome was comparatively civilised under Julius Caesar, but under successive emperors it descended into a degenerate society. This was due to Greek and Roman cultures copying what was worst in each and abandoning what was best. Vice and immorality reigned and all that was good in human nature that early Christianity embodied, was looked at contemptuously. Family life was once revered and divorce unknown for half a century. Under the new Empire it was mocked. Women married in order to be divorced, and lived out their lives by discarding their husbands or being discarded by them. A growing stoicism championed suicide as a way out of misfortune. No love or compassion was shown towards other unfortunates. However, Christian men and women were showing love and hope even from the confines of the catacombs.

Physical factors

From the outset a man's greater physical strength and a woman's child-bearing role were factors that determined where authority lay. A man was a hunter and a protector. A woman was a carer. As populations and know-how increased a man became the breadwinner; the fighter of wars. Women were responsible for chores, and helped to grow things within the limits of their strength. Man was still supreme in construction and carrying heavier loads. Women were preoccupied with pregnancy and child-rearing. So customs developed from these circumstances.

The raw side of man inclined him to ill-treat women. In warfare women on the vanquished ones' side were invariably raped and slaughtered. In various parts of the world women were the objects of polygamy and polyandry. In some societies wives are bought, extended families dominate them, and educational attainments are disregarded.

Chivalry

Social conscience, corporate consensus, and Christian religious influence combined to introduce a sense of chivalry in some societies. This custom was evidenced in the behaviour of mediaeval knights in jousting, women and children first on the Titanic, and surrendering seats on the Clapham omnibus. Women were not, at first, pressed or conscripted. These advantages were more than outweighed by educational disadvantages, the stigma of illegitimacy, lack of suffrage, and unfair inheritance laws.

In Sikhism the gurus' teaching enthused in the Sikhs a great spirit of chivalry. They rescued 15,000 Maratha women from the clutches of Ahmad Shah Abdali, who had enslaved them for taking to Iran. But the Sikhs at great risk to their own lives rescued them and delivered each one of them to her home. Cunningham rightly calls it "the greatest act of chivalry in the East". In fact, the Sikhs are not allowed to exercise proprietary rights over women captured in battle. It is on record that the Begum of the Governor of Bassi Pathanan fell into the hands of the Sikhs. Ajit Singh, the Guru's son himself escorted her back to the enemy's camp, and while she stayed with the Sikhs she was treated as a sister.

Exceptions

I can personally vouch for an exception to the subjugation of women in society. In what was known as the British Cameroons, and to some extent in parts of Nigeria, women had economic power on account of their strong character and trading acumen. The indigenous population was subject to a benign colonial administration and most Cameroonian men were either skilled tradesmen or labourers. Their pay was so low that they were obliged to eat on credit until the end of each month. The suppliers of food were the women known colloquially as "chop mammies". Their hold on the economy was such that even bandits did not dare to hijack payrolls even though money had to be transported in Land Rovers all over the country. There was only one bank building. I transported large sums of cash through the bush at the end of each month. This was for payrolls of civil engineering projects. I changed my route regularly but it made no difference. The drums beat through the bush and it was known where I was at every point. The "chop mammies" were protecting their business interests. Who said women had no power? On the other hand the takings of John Holt and Unilever stores were considered to be fair game as these were transported to the bank. In Nigeria the same principles applied in the bush and in large cities such as Lagos and Ibadan women were prominent in general trading, especially in selling the wonderful native cloth.

Philosophy

Aristotle, the philosopher, thought women an agreeable blunder and an erroneous development. He taught that woman was less complete, less courageous, weaker and more impulsive than a man. Dante said that like laymen, women may learn a little Latin but not more. In Hindu thought there are references to women in the Vedas where so much is made of celibacy and it is thought married men cannot aspire to communion with God or lead a saintly or pure life. Women were excluded from religious functions. Women were not, at one stage, allowed to listen to the Vedas, although there is ample evidence that most of the songs in the Vedas were composed by women.

It is alleged that the Apostle Paul was influenced by contemporary Greek philosophy and possibly by oriental custom. I think too much has been read into this. The long history of mankind has been paved by the mistreatment of women. Her inferiority has stemmed, in some circles, from the manner in which the fall was blamed upon Eve. It has been suggested that this was Paul's opinion: that his teaching that it was not good to touch a woman, and his preference for an unmarried state for widows and all the unmarried, indicated a streak of misogyny in his make-up. These assessments are probably unfair, but his views in this respect do line up with philosophers' writings and with customs of his day: in fact, more closely than is apparent when weighing his isolated statements about women with the whole weight of his other writing. I will return to this when discussing the treatment of women in religion.

Safety valves

Ordinary people are often prisoners of culture, but their resilience enables them to escape by inventing customs, and resorting to humour. When Britain became over-populated and crime was rife a social remedy was to deport people to Australia for the most minor of offences. There were over 300 offences that incurred the death penalty. A woman aged sixty-three was sentenced in 1791 to seven years' transportation for stealing table linen. A man was sentenced to seven years' penal servitude and seven years' police supervision for stealing onions. One could, however, escape punishment by a legal fiction known as pleading the benefit of the clergy. That was being able to recite a prayer. On the other hand the only escape from a charge of "heresy" was to recant one's own opinion.

Irish Catholics overcame social problems arising from anti-family planning teachings by marrying late. They also avoided getting too ardent about the mystic side of their religion by joking about it. They explained to me that theirs was a different culture from that of English Protestants. The religious, such as monks and nuns, followed such an austere and serious life that they would let off steam when on leave or in less formal moments. I remember a large nun enjoying a pint of beer with relatives and nobody else thinking it was anything out of the ordinary. My own uncle was a famous monk, in fact the head of an august order. Years after his death I heard stories about his sense of humour. It is only appropriate to relate instances concerning women, which is a pity.

In nunnery there are various levels of commitment and status. For example Dominican nuns of the Third Order were really recruited to do menial work. They were skivvies. In the course of an inspection of a Catholic special residential school I had a charming interview with a mother superior. (As an aside, we were both admirers of Billy Graham.) She related how, after a preaching visit of my uncle, she went into the kitchen and, to her surprise, heard a nun of the Third Order singing a strange song. It went – O, Jemima look at your uncle Jim. He's in the duck pond learning how to swim. First he tries the left stroke and then he tries the right. Then he treads on a bar of soap and skids right out of sight. She remonstrated…Sister, Sister, have you taken leave of your senses? Whereupon, there came a triumphant answer that the Father Provincial had taught her that. My uncle was a highly liked and respected person who kept to his commitment and vows to the end. It was a great embarrassment to him that he was stalked everywhere by a wealthy spinster. On one occasion she jumped over the altar rails and prostrated herself at his feet. Underlying this incident there was a deeper sorrow that the rigid rules relating to sex and marriage in orthodoxy are responsible for much unhappiness and personal instability. My uncle was full of fun and we loved him dearly as children. On visits home he would grasp our thighs just above the knee until it was painful. He would say that it was a cow bite. My mother used to serve hot buttered scones that for some reason we called "fat rascals". But he renamed them "sticky devils". In my childish mind I used to imagine Jesus relaxing and engaging in humour in that lovely home in Bethany after escaping from his arduous ministry for a few days.

Orders of nuns in America are diversifying. They are branching out from their traditional roles to serve society more generally. They have discarded their habits (i.e. their uniform) and in one instance are running an establishment that helps men beat drug addiction. The Vatican is seeking to bring these nuns under former disciplines. The nuns consider the Vatican to be remote and out of touch with cultural changes in American Catholicism. It would seem that the nuns have a vision to follow the teachings of Jesus.

Technology

A new Roman Catholic archbishop has drawn media attention by his remarks about the affect of the internet upon younger people. In his wide experience he has witnessed the breakdown of corporate relationships by overuse of remote electronic means of communication.

Extreme withdrawal from face-to-face human contact has led to suicides. Girls can be groomed by the deceptions of paedophiles on the net. This can stem from youngsters being closeted alone for hours rather than attending youth clubs or mixing with friends.

Certainly the advent of television, computer games, and iPods, has transformed attitudes, employment, fashions, and sexual behaviour. Fewer co-habiting people are getting married, more people are getting into debt, and the divide between those who are selfish and those who seek to love their neighbours is getting wider. Political corruption and political correctness are reaching levels that are threatening the very core of genuine democracy.

The media is having an unwelcome affect on girls and young women by its digital retouching of images. The custom of airbrushing whereby models are shown as artificially perfect is undermining the esteem of girls as young as seven. Thin body images lead to increases in anorexia. These can also add to the bullying of obese children and their exclusion from friendship circles.

Drugs and crime

In the past drinking excessive quantities of alcohol was probably the most serious cause of degeneration in Western society. This led to the formulation of Temperance societies which are now defunct. In the Far East opium-taking or smoking ruined the lives of millions. A more recent phenomenon in the West has been an influx of all kinds of drugs ranging from cannabis, to cocaine, and drugs causing "highs" such as ecstasy. Money is such a big factor in society, and so much money is made by drugs barons and by those who are involved in the sexual exploitation of women that failure to clamp down on such activities by authorities gives grounds for disquiet.

Moral decline and discrimination

The legalisation of lotteries and casinos generates money for the operators but it creates untold misery and addictive behaviour on the part of the participants. Elderly women often prefer to go to bingo rather than the women's fellowships. The breakdown of family relationships means that many old people lead lonely lives. The quality of customs and culture deteriorate as people get more and more materialistic and selfish. Moral standards decline and the world is going back to a state akin to that of Noah's day – eat, drink and be merry, for tomorrow we die. Educational standards and our deposit of knowledge are on an upward curve, yet this has not resulted in greater happiness. Higher moral standards, sounder ethics, and the pursuit of righteousness will serve society much better: sadly these are being neglected.

The elderly are being exploited by dishonest workmen and by mail-order scams offering illusive cash prizes. Pension allocations are derisory particularly to widows, and ordinary people suffer from the greed and incompetence of banks and investment fund managers. Governments fail to regulate adequately.

Feminism

Harriet Harman, a British cabinet member responsible for equality, has started to champion the cause of her own sex in rather an avant garde way. Her seniority places her in the position of Deputy Prime Minister. In his absence on holiday she is running the country. She thinks that if more women were involved at top levels within institutions there would be greater transparency and effectiveness. She reckoned that if Lehman Brothers had been Lehman Sisters the bank might have escaped closure. Her comments attracted an immediate backlash from both men and women. Even a spokesperson of the Fawcett Society, a feminist organisation, thought she had put her foot where her mouth was. It was also interesting for several reasons. Although she could have put her case more diplomatically, there might have been a more balanced reaction on the part of the media. Women are not fairly represented in top-level positions: only about four per cent are to be found in boardrooms. Harriet's stance highlights my distinction between equality, for the sake of it, which Harriet seemed to be advocating, and complete impartiality. Quotas may be a means of achieving parity quickly but such a route can hardly be in the public interest. The British Labour Party proposes to operate a quota system favouring women in the selection of its Parliamentary candidates. The agitated reaction of some male MP's was an indication of the heat that the subject of feminism generates. Even as I am writing the Sunday papers have launched frivolous attacks on Harriet's political performance. For instance she has been accused of driving herself to a war hero's funeral. It is alleged that if she had gone in an official car she could have been working on state papers. Current chat shows have made a lot of the topic and views about the place of women vary widely. There is even a lobby that claims men are being persecuted!

I will be returning to this topic when I debate what prospects there are for women in the future. As to government and banking Harriet Harman considers that men cannot safely be left to run things on their own. She was accused, unfairly, of seeking to guarantee her future position. A man she succeeded objected, stating that equality cannot be dictated, which was fair, as was his admission that she had beaten four men by her talent, but he added that it was nothing to do with her gender. A PR consultant denied that talent was paramount. The most important thing was using men and women together since they had different attributes. Does not this bring us back to the fact that God created a woman to be man's companion and not his skivvy? Harriet has certainly boosted women's rights on such issues as childcare and flexible working hours. She is aiming to extend the period of statutory maternity leave.

Family breakdown

Women and men are being affected by a materialistic society. Women are juggling pregnancies and child-rearing with careers and jobs. Men are often the losers in child custody cases. I will be following up the changing scene when discussing government attempts to move towards greater enforcement of equality. The recent recession has driven tens of thousands out of work and families are having their homes repossessed. Very often women are retaining their jobs because they are lower paid and men are on the scrap heap. There is some evidence that women are behaving heroically in this crisis and winning greater respect. It is well established that in the bitter years between 1926 and 1932 it was the Welsh women who kept families together through the coal mining depression. Thus the spirit of the people, good or bad, is the driver for change in custom and culture in the same way that codified law is so often the result of past practice.

People can be held down by governments, exploited, and manipulated but by degrees up-swells of public opinion can turn tyrannies upside down. Wonderful instances are the fall of the Berlin Wall and the overthrow of dictators in the Balkans. There are currently undercurrents of dissatisfaction in the ranks of the Christian Church about over-authoritarianism and bias against women. Hopefully, there will shortly be another great up-swell of a spiritual nature.

Chapter Thirteen

WOMEN, FAITHS, AND SOCIETY

"The moving finger writes; and, having writ,
moves on: nor all thy Piety nor Wit
shall lure it back to cancel half a line,
nor all thy tears wash out a Word of it."
Rubaiyat of Omar Khayyam. Edward Fitzgerald.

Analysis

Neither religion nor society can be said, generally, to have favoured women over the course of history. Latterly, in most democracies the lot of women has improved significantly within society, but there has not been the same rate of favourable progress in the Christian Church. I have been made aware of an interesting exception to these trends in another religion. In this case women are treated equally but this does not mean that this freedom has been matched in the society in which they live. I have already made a brief reference to Sikhism in chapter 12, and now, looking into this race of people in detail, and being advised by a knowledgeable member of that religion, I can pass on fascinating information. The conduct of society is, everywhere, at the mercy of man's fallen nature and behaviour-swings are slow and unpredictable. However, in religion it is notionally possible for the lot of women to be changed for the good almost instantaneously. If leaders were gracious and genuine shepherds they could change the lot of woman at will. To bring about such change within Christianity all that would be required is for men to agree to do God's will on earth rather than following their own version of what this should be.

Sikhism

Sikhism differs from Hinduism. It is not a polytheistic faith and in this respect is in line with Judaism, Christianity and Islam. It is a relatively young religion being about 500 years old. From the outset its gurus brought in teachings that sought to make women equal. This was both courageous and enlightening especially as Indian society at the time discriminated against women. It was within the power of gurus to liberate women spiritually as, for that matter, such power is in the hands of all religious leaders. Then Guru Nanak (1469-1539) appeared. He taught that women equally shared the grace of God. He rejected a contemporary view that women were spiritually tainted. Women were not something that was inferior to men. Women should sit side by side with men in religious gatherings and enjoy equal status. Women were allowed to lead religious congregations, to take part in the recital of the Holy Scriptures, to work as priests and preachers, and to be involved in all religious, cultural, social, political and secular activities. Not long ago the leaders of the Sikh Temple at Smethwick were inefficient and the women took over control for a period. Women can join the Panch Pyaras and perform Kirtan, solemnise marriage, and work as teachers, doctors, lawyers and judges. Distinctions between men and women have been abolished. It does not escape my attention that all gurus are men.

Indian society

It should not be implied that modern India still resembles descriptions of its society throughout history. Most of the information given here has been derived from articles written by historians prior to 1975, and I have had to rely on their writing. Readers should allow that historical facts do not explain underlying causes. These are invariably of an economic or political nature. In England there were times when people could be hanged for comparatively minor offences and little children were sent up chimneys to sweep them. It should also be noted, however, that the position of women in Indian society has been different from that of women in the Western world. The point has already been made that Sikh women have always enjoyed parity with men in religion. It is possible that their position in society might have been better if Sikhs were not a minority nation in India. The following are historic examples of the status of women in India as it was. The field includes what is now India, Pakistan, and Bangladesh.

Satee, and the Caste System The gurus were up against the customs of Indian Society which proved too powerful for them to be able to effect significant changes. They were, however, quick to condemn barbarous customs such as Satee. This is a practice whereby the widow was burnt alive on her husband's funeral pyre. The Hindu belief in reincarnation gives privileges to those who are "second born". From the Brahmins down there is a structure of class system with the untouchables at the bottom. This impacts on men and women alike, and, therefore, is subsidiary to my subject.

Girl Siblings At one time the birth of a girl was not regarded as a happy event, whereas the birth of a boy was celebrated. In Punjabi society a second girl was, not infrequently, killed at birth, infanticide being condoned as far as females were concerned. The custom concerning dowry meant that the bride's side of a family had a large financial burden. Higher caste families sometimes found it difficult to find suitable husbands. It is fair to state that once a baby girl was accepted she was treated equally with a boy.

Arranged Marriages an entrenched custom in Indian society is one of arranged marriages. Prior to marriage a woman was guarded by her mother and older women of her father's household. She was chaperoned so that her good name would help in marriage negotiations. As a young unmarried woman, especially if educated, she was expected to contribute towards household expenses, save towards her own dowry, and in any case to do chores. These might be looking after younger siblings, cooking and cleaning. Parents alerted their kin network to look out for a suitable match. It was not uncommon for spouses to be distant relatives. Negotiations were at one time opened by the family barber. Later (and nowadays) both the bride and the groom were seen and interviewed by relatives on both sides and it was normal practice to see each other prior to marriage. It is not always appreciated that both parties had the right to refuse any proposed match and frequently did so. These customs have become eroded but there are instances within immigrant communities of so-called honour killings. In such cases the killers have to face the penalties of the law.

Brides There are numerous customs and religious rites, varying according to religion, relating to marriage and fertility rites that are not relevant to my subject. The first days of marriage were difficult for a new bride. She sat, veiled, in a corner and her husband's female relatives inspected her and commented on her looks and complexion. They also passed judgment on what she had brought as her dowry. On marriage a woman was incorporated into her husband's descent group. A man remained throughout his life a member of his father's descent group (patrilineal descent) but a woman made a gradual transition from the descent from her father to that of her husband. It is only after her death that a woman achieved status of her husband's descent group. Very quickly she was expected to bear the brunt of the household chores.

Polyandry Hindus and Sikhs generally had an exogamous descent system while the Muslim system was generally endogamous: this means that Hindus and Sikhs gave their women to other men outside the descent group, but Muslims retained their own women within the descent group. Polyandry means a relationship in which a number of men hold common sexual rights in a single woman. In Hindu-Sikh socicty the men were often brothers and the term "adelphic polyandry" was employed. There is uncertainty as to whether these situations amounted to polygamous "marriage" and one sociologist used the term "polykoity". This information dates up to the year 1975. There were cultural reasons for these practices connected with dwindling land resources. Migration to Britain has to a large extent solved the problem, but not in a few cases of arranged marriages and honour killings. Previously other devices were meant to maintain basic economic solvency. In Western society there was once a system of primogeniture. The oldest son inherited the farm to ensure that it was not split up, which would be the case if inheritance went equally to all siblings.

Exploitation

It has been necessary to give a brief outline of the role of women in Indian society over a long period of time in order to emphasise their subjection and what sort of lives they had to endure. Guru Nanak was a breath of fresh air and a spiritual liberator. I am deeply concerned that in Christianity in the past women had no such spiritual parity. Today they are not treated as equals by a majority of men within denominations. There is much that has been done and can be done to address problems of gender within world society. The world and the Church founded on Jesus Christ are within two distinct spheres. The former are the kingdoms of the world and the latter is the Kingdom of God. I can hope that all nations will follow paths of more civilised rectitude; that statutory powers will be exercised more righteously. Historically nations have adopted various attitudes towards the rights of women and these still do. Modernism and post-modernism have made strides in opposing discrimination. I can but protest and express my sorrow as to the treatment of women by those who profess to run God's vineyard, and refuse to run it on principles of divine love and impartiality.

Adam's problem

In the Judeo-Christian Book of Genesis it is recorded that God forbade Adam to eat the forbidden fruit. When Adam disobeyed he blamed Eve, saying, "The woman whom thou gavest to be with me, she gave me of the tree, and I did eat." There is even a hint that it was partly God's fault for producing the woman. What kind of a man is that, obviously a fallen and manipulating one? Surely, if a man is supposed to be so superior he should have taken all the blame on the chin even though Eve was partly to blame. Unfortunately, the writer of Genesis, the great Moses, did not see fit to express such a view about this sad debacle. Although ignored by many there is a Biblical qualification that every man is born of a woman. Moses was a great prophet but all prophets are subject to their own spirit as well as being inspired by the Holy Spirit. This episode was used ever after as an excuse to subjugate women and deny them of their equal rights before God. Its legacy was carried over by those who chose to interpret the New Testament writings to suit their own case. Happily, it did not negate the wonderful message of repentance towards God and faith in the Lord Jesus, or obscure the truths of the cross and the resurrection.

Nanak's humility

Here was a man who was unfamiliar with the Christian gospel but was so generous of spirit that his innate decency and great mind compelled him to treat people as equals regardless of biological differences. His views in this respect cry out to all of us to forget unnecessary theological, macho-inspired arguments and use our intelligence and listen to our own consciences. Nanak was unable to influence the society in which he lived as much as he would have wished. But he gave women such a wonderful sense of freedom of spirit in their religion that nobody could deprive them of this granted liberation. Turning to Christianity again, it seems to me, it is not only the women who are being deprived but God himself is being deprived as well of their fullness of worship and service.

Islam

Islam allowed considerable concessions to women. Prophet Mohammed meticulously laid down the rights of women to the property of their parents and husbands. It is he who emphatically declared that acquisition of knowledge is an incumbent on every male and female. It is clear to outsiders from this major world faith that there are vastly different factions within Islam today and vastly differing interpretations of the Holy Koran just as there are, similarly, factions within Christianity. For example, factions within Islam are against the education of women and there are moderate imams who distinguish between the Koran and the Hadith and allow for the effect of culture. Currently more women are graduating from universities in Saudi Arabia than men although women are more restricted in that society than in some Islamic countries where there is secular government. On being asked on television why Muslim women could go about Britain unescorted, an imam explained the old rule against this practice was in order to ensure their protection in more lawless times. Of course in the Islamic faith women are not allowed to utter the call to prayer (Azan) or to become a priest (imam). Islamic society is heavily influenced by the teachings of the Holy Koran. Women are disallowed to override views of their husbands and dominate in any way. (Ulnissa 4-34) The testimony of two women is equal to that of one man. (ii: 282)

There are both moderate and fundamentalist Imams and the latter do not, unfortunately, get as much publicity in Western media as extremists. For example, Sheikh Mohammed Sayyid Tantawi is a moderate voice at the apex of Sunni Islam. He has condemned terrorism and the full face veil. He is the Grand Mufti of Egypt and Grand Sheikh of Al-Azhar. As attitudes towards women hardened he supported their rights. In particular he declared that senior government and legal positions should be open to them. He wanted easier divorce for women and favoured abortion in cases of rape. The practice of wearing the *hijab* began to decline in middle-class Egyptian society but from 1980 and onwards, particularly amongst students, it was significantly on the increase. Young women were wearing the full face veil to show greater modesty and devotion or to protect themselves from sexual harassment. Government saw this as a support for fundamentalist Islam. He issued a *fatwa* allowing girls to go uncovered in France in support of that country's ban on the *hijab* in schools. Visiting a secondary school in Cairo he found a girl wearing a *hijab* and removed it from her. I am mentioning the stance of this eminent cleric to show that there is a breadth in attitudes within Islam just as there is within Christianity.

Then there was the Grand Ayatollah Mohammed Fadlallah whose political views caused the West to brigade him with terrorist sympathisers, although he openly opposed the Twin Tower attacks. He was highly respected in Islam. He was a moderate as far as women were concerned, teaching that they should work and have a right to strike their husbands if in an abusive relationship. He issued a *fatwa* supporting this. He opposed female circumcision and so-called "honour killings". Other Islamic leaders are more hard-line and even oppose the education of women.

On the other hand there has always been a consistency throughout Sikhism. Sikh Guru Nanak restored women to full rights and privileges enjoyed by men. He tried to raise them from depths of degradation to the heights of glory. He conferred on her the title "Daughter of God" (I have already shown that in real Christianity a woman is actually a "Son of God" through the Holy Spirit). He swept away the age-old threadbare and derogatory terminology used to malign women. In the compositions of the gurus it is clearly mentioned that God is the creator of both men and women, and He has created all the relations. Therefore all have their own rights. For this reason no prejudices should exist regarding the superiority or inferiority of anyone.

Other religions

Judaism I have written about women in the Old Testament already. I note that there were two factions in those times: Pharisees and Sadducees. Once the sacrifices ceased with the destruction of the Temple by the Romans in AD 71 all religious reasons for excluding women would seem to have vanished. However, it was only in relatively modern times that two different factions emerged: orthodox and liberal (or modern rabbinical). In the liberal wing there are women rabbis. This compares with the broad Christian Church where orthodoxy excludes women and liberal, Pentecostal, Methodist and the Salvation Army treat women as equal to men. I pay tribute to the Jewish woman. Much of Jewish religion is centred on the family. The Passover is celebrated in households just as it was immediately prior to the Exodus. Jewish mothers are great matriarchal upholders of their families.

Until the advent of Nebuchadnezzar Israel was a theocracy and so the natures of society, culture and religion were intertwined with one another. This continued to have an aftermath. That is why even the early Christian Church was influenced by Jewish tradition. In a dissimilar way there are differences of traditional influence within Islam according to whether a country is secular or governed by mullahs.

Buddhism I simply note that the monastic system is almost exclusively for males. I have never seen a lady Buddhist monk but there is nothing in the tenets to suggest whether women should be included or excluded. There is an element of nothingness.

Christian Science I only mention this sect for two reasons. It is world-wide with over 3,000 branches around the world and it was founded by a women: Mary Baker Eddy, born 1821.

Testing the spirits

I ask, "Is it right to take any notice of other faiths? Can and should we be prepared to learn anything from these?" Looking at the largest group of Christians, the orthodox churches, one can trace a change of attitude towards other religions. At one time, as far as the Vatican was concerned, all other religions, or for that matter other Christian denominations, were condemned as "false religions". The Second Vatican Council of 1962 ruled differently. Its documents on page 662 make it clear that other religions strive to answer the restless strivings of human hearts by proposing ways which consist of teaching, rules of life and sacred ceremonies. It adds properly that Jesus is the way the truth and the life...these (other religions) reflect rays of that truth which enlightens all men. Now for the first time there is recognition of other religions as entities with which the Church should enter into dialogue. I believe that it is not necessary to import their doctrinal beliefs at the expense of plain Biblical teaching. However, I think I have demonstrated quite forcibly that Christians can learn a lot about the correct treatment of women in religion by studying the views of Guru Nanak.

Relevance to the main case

The most relevant point to the main study of the case of women in the Christian Church that has emerged in this chapter is that a different religion grasped the nettle from the outset. This demonstrates that there is nothing to prevent an immediate adoption of correct spiritual behaviour in religion. This principle is at variance with actuality in a majority of cases in Christianity. The example of Guru Nanak's teaching is a beacon of hope to Christian women worldwide.

It is also salutary that in varied cultures with their different customs women, gradually, have either been more recognised as equals, or not at all. It seems anomalous that in Indian society women's rights have not progressed as quickly as in the Western world although in the Sikh religion these have been accepted totally: conversely, women have had a raw deal in many sections of the Christian Church.

Chapter Fourteen

EMANCIPATION OF WOMEN

And if I pray the only prayer
That moves my lips for me
Is, 'Leave the heart that now I bear,
And give me liberty!'

Emily Brontë from "The Old Stoic".

A gradual process

An historical perspective of the treatment of women and of women's suffrage will show that woman was downtrodden by man for thousands of years. Her social liberation, particularly in democracies, progressed rapidly from the beginning of the twentieth century and is continuing. In the Christian Church, however, the rightful recognition of women stagnated except in relatively new and mainly independent denominations. The Catholic Church gave lip service to women in 1962, as I shall relate, but still excluded them from officiating in its sacramental system. In my personal opinion the women were fortunate! It is not possible, or even appropriate to my subject, to provide a detailed history of women's emancipation in society. I will confine myself to a combination of broad-brush historical events and isolated examples. As the welcome social liberation of women proceeds apace, with its statutory enforcements, there is a danger that both men and women will be deprived of their own spaces, and this would be as much of a mistake as is the present misguided political correctness.

Women's suffrage

It was only in the nineteenth century that women began to fight actively for their rights. They began to strive for equality in suffrage, education, property rights and the professions. This lead was evidenced first in Western Europe and North America and suffrage experienced the first breakthrough. Women got the vote in Britain as late as 1928. In New Zealand it was in 1893 and Australia 1902. In the USA it was 1920. In France it was in 1944. Russian women got the vote in 1917, the year of the Revolution, and in China it was 1947.

In the Middle East, Yemen granted her women the right to vote in 1971 and by this date Jordan, Kuwait, Saudi Arabia, and Nigeria (Northern Region) had not granted the vote to their women. In 1945, when the United Nations was formed about half of its fifty-one member countries had not granted the vote to its women. Even by 1973, women had no vote and were not eligible for election in nearly ten per cent of the member states.

The beginning of the twentieth century was an outstanding era for suffragette protest in Britain. Protesters were arrested, imprisoned, went on hunger strike and were force-fed. One of them threw herself in front of the King's (Edward VII) horse at Tattenham Corner during the Derby at Epson. She was killed. Emmeline Pankhurst inspired the militancy. She emerged, finally, victorious but remained relatively unpopular with the establishment. She was refused membership of the Independent Labour Party on the grounds of gender despite being a friend of Kier Hardy. It is likely, if history lasts much longer, that she will have a better place in posterity than her opponents. In fact, in 1999 *Time* placed her in the top 100 most important people of the twentieth century. She died in the same year as women won the vote and her statue was erected in Victoria Tower Gardens two years later. She was far from perfect but it must be allowed that neither is any other human being. This is something that is a blind-spot in religion.

Women and education

The first Education Act for women in Britain was passed in 1906. This was largely as a result of the emergence of women academics becoming known as "the blue stockings". Their history can be traced from 1860 to 1939 (the outbreak of World War 2). Women were allowed into certain universities, could sit examinations, but could not have degrees conferred upon them. By 1939 they were treated equally, University College London leading, but not so in Cambridge. It was not until after the passing of the National Health Act, in 1947, female medical students were admitted to every London teaching hospital. Before then they were confined to the Royal Free Hospital which only admitted women. This severely restricted opportunity. It has been related that in 1899 at Manchester University women medical students were required to eat their lunch in the dissecting room so as not to distract the "real" doctors. One Cambridge professor on walking into a lecture theatre, to find only women present, walked out as "there was nobody there".

All kinds of psychological barriers were raised against the education of women ranging from claims that it was a health hazard causing sterility, to opinions that a woman's brain was 5oz (50g) lighter than a man's and thus reduced her mental capacity. At Durham in 1899 female students were regarded as either having devious minds or being nervous wrecks. It took outstanding and courageous women to break into areas dominated by men. Such a person was Dr Elizabeth Garrett Anderson who has a famous London hospital named after her. In citing names of famous women I realise it is inevitable that many other worthy people are still omitted. I will mention Nurse Edith Cavell and Florence Nightingale and Odette Churchill and Marie Curie. Before becoming Britain's first Prime Minister, Margaret Thatcher was Secretary of State for Education for three years. During that time she saved the Open University and laid down a framework for the expansion of education.

Prior to the nineteenth century girls were not given formal education: only the rich had private tutors. Jews did not admit girls into rabbinical schools. Muslim women were not allowed to attend mosque schools. In India education was restricted only to the twice-born or the upper strata of Hindu Society.

Women in society

Because of restricted access to education wealthy young women did not have employment and it was customary for their parents or themselves to look for good marriage prospects. Lower-class girls went into domestic service or nursing. After the Industrial Revolution they worked in very poor conditions and for low pay in mills and factories. The average size family was several times higher than the present-day norm. Life expectancy was as low as forty (this was still the level in West Africa in the mid-twentieth century!). Even as women secured more recognition they were paid less than men for the same job and were obliged to retire earlier. They were not regarded as equal to men when applying for jobs. Therefore it was very rare to have a female in top or senior posts in the public sector. Lady Astor became the first woman Member of Parliament in Britain as late as the twentieth century. Remarkably there had been several female monarchs starting with Mary Tudor as early as 1553.

Worldwide social conditions always worsened with conquests, particularly in India with the resulting chaos and confusion women suffered most. The position of women in India was secondary and submissive to men. Polygamy was legal. Widows were not allowed to remarry but were forced to burn themselves on the funeral pyres of their husbands. Female migrants to the New World and Australasia endured all kinds of hardship. Jewish women suffered from pogroms in countries like Russia and Spain. Being the weaker sex they were less able to escape genocides.

The invention of the typewriter and stenography opened up opportunities for women as secretaries, and this was followed by punched card accounting, and ultimately word processing. In two world wars (1914-1918 and 1939-1945) women worked in factories and were finally conscripted into female counterparts of the three armed services. Women became spies and secret agents.

The yoke

Since the twelfth century nuns were kept cloistered. I can vouch that this was still so in the 1930s. I was taught by nuns from the age of four until I was eight. I was an altar boy in a convent and two itinerant donation collecting nuns had a rendezvous at our house once a year where they could eat in isolation in the parlour. The nuns needed permission from the Mother Superior before having outside contacts. All communications both incoming and outgoing were subject to scrutiny. It was tantamount to being imprisoned both physically and mentally. The Second Vatican Council called for changes. Nuns should be involved in the work of the lay apostolate and be encouraged, when suitable, to enter higher education. It is possible that change was influenced by the earlier work of José Escriva the founder of Opus Dei. His vision was for recognition of the work of the laity. It is probable that increased educational standards and public opinion had the biggest influence in bringing about change. I must emphasise that in the past allegations of impropriety were generally proved to be false and malicious. The history of Maria Monk is a good example.

Ordinary Catholics were dominated by clerics until the 1960s. They were banned from taking part in the services and prayers of "false religions". Therefore as a Catholic soldier I was unable to accept an offer from a Methodist that we should attend each other's churches as a "taster". My sister failed to obtain a dispensation to be a bridesmaid at her best friend's Baptist church. The fact is that change came about not so much as an internal liberation policy but because the media widened public knowledge and also that today most Catholics are not prepared to be dictated to or to readily obey childish rules. Clerics were afraid of their own shadows. Now that attitudes have changed enormously we have cases of people leaving the Anglican Church for Rome on the grounds that some Anglican bishops do not seem to believe the fundamental Christian message any longer. They say there was no virgin birth, no literal resurrection, and that supernatural events were myths. Rome believes and teaches these things convincingly. My personal view is that such converts are very genuine. However, they are too ready to tolerate a lot of extra-Biblical teaching based on tradition and to adopt a doctrine of salvation by works, which is not the complete spiritual emancipation they hope for. They do not bother that they are entering a church that has scant regard for the spiritual rights of women.

Breaking the yoke

Access to unfettered information and education for all, enabled women to think for themselves and to become more aware of what other women were doing. I have referred elsewhere to patterns of nunnery and instances of breakaway groups of nuns. However, there has been a marked increase of nuns who have left their "vocation" altogether. Studies in America showed that since the Second Vatican Council of 1962 there has been an increase in disaffiliation. Although it was theoretically possible to get dispensation from one's vows it was not socially acceptable to the Catholic community and this virtually prohibited change. In 1960 only 765 American nuns out of 168,527 left their orders. In 1966 as many as 2,000 defected, a number that reached its peak in 1970 when 4,337 exited. After that the numbers declined but this was due to the fact that recruitment dropped sharply and that those who intended to leave had done so earlier.

Some good research has been done about ex-nuns in society and this is very relevant to the discovery of outcomes of emancipation. A confraternity of the Order of the Sacred Heart left Rome en masse. In San Pedro the hierarchy fell out with another convent community because it diversified by running a rehabilitation unit for male alcoholics. Those who stayed in enjoyed a degree of emancipation including the right to adopt modern dress in place of the old habits. Some who left agonised about their decision and others experienced hostility from their parents. A majority had a great sense of freedom and a welcome realisation of personal individualism. Very few left the Catholic Church. In fact a different study found that only a small percentage of numerous Catholics who disaffected did so for doctrinal reasons. The commonest reasons were materialism and the Church's opposition to family planning and abortion. Ex-nuns often had uneasy times of transition but adapted well in the long run; finding satisfactory places in external adult life.

Women in the Church

I have dealt with this subject more fully elsewhere. In this context, ordinary female Church members, on the whole, have not advanced their position. Until 1970 women could not be ordained in the Church of England. Despite organised resistance against it, women were ordained, and there are factions who still refuse to recognise them. There is an ongoing heated debate about whether women can be bishops. I will return to this subject.

In orthodoxy there has been no ordination of women and there is no debate about the subject within the Church. Therefore, any woman must leave these churches if she is convinced she has a call to ministerial service. This is good for them because they not only achieve personal emancipation from over-authoritarian systems: they can become a true priest to God in a Biblical sense. The Roman Church is suffering setbacks in South America where defections to Pentecostalism are accelerating to such an extent that it is being claimed that new charismatic churches are opening all over the place. It is leading to an increasing liberation of women. This poses also a question of whether too sudden and too much independence leads to inadequately trained oversights, and badly taught people. This is not a criticism of Pentecostal doctrine. Implications are discussed in Part III.

Individualism

Is the pendulum swinging too far away from authority and travelling towards unfettered individualism? Those with free spirits think that opponents of total religious freedom are afraid of losing their ability to remain six feet above criticism in a pulpit. Conversely, those who are still fettered by religiosity are afraid that their own -isms will be tested, tried and challenged in the court of general opinion. Two threats to the prospective full emancipation of women in religion are the apathy of women themselves and their inherent brainwashing by others. The interesting Vatican II documents paid tribute to women but did not move an inch to improve their lot spiritually. On the subject of social justice these documents condemned every type of discrimination exercised on grounds of sex or religion. This must be eradicated as contrary to God's intent. "For in truth it must still be regretted that fundamental personal rights are not yet being personally honoured. Such is the case of a woman who is denied the right to choose a husband, to embrace a state of life, or to acquire an education or cultural benefits equal to those recognised for men." Although this is admirable it is also a case of the pot calling the kettle black! Why did the documents not add a warning to women to keep off the established sacramental grass? This is what they are still required to do.

A closing message in the Vatican II documents addressed to women of all states – "girls, wives, mothers, and widows recognise that women constituted half of the immense human family. The church was proud to have glorified and liberated women and to have brought into relief her basic equality with man. But the hour is coming, in fact has come, when the vocation of women is being achieved in all its fullness...so deep a transformation, women impregnated with the spirit of the gospel can do much to aid mankind in not falling." The message goes on to pour praise on women for the traditional roles they have always undertaken. This was little more than lip service because actual male dominance in spiritual matters has not changed at all.

Orthodoxy has glorified women after they are dead; a task they should leave to God. It has not liberated women spiritually one iota and not recognised their equality with men, so the writer of this message was not being strictly honourable. The hour has not yet come!

I am going to deal in the following chapter with two sets of four cases in which giving religious freedom to women had different outcomes. In one set women were gloriously successful in the dissemination of a true gospel and in the other it brought the sincerity of the gospel under a degree of suspicion. I will interpose and alternate these cases so as not to be putting all the negative news together. I will come to a conclusion.

A late insert

Just as this book was completed there was a new development. Following a vote in the Church of England Synod to ordain women as bishops the Roman Catholic Congregation for the Doctrine of the Faith declared that the ordination of women as Roman Catholic bishops was a "crime against the faith" and would be subject to discipline. The folly of this decision will become apparent. It will result in the eventual polarisation of stubborn and insensitive religionists. Temporarily these will survive only because of the tolerance of those whom they offend. No doubt the Pope will be politely welcomed by a gracious Queen of England this year despite the fact that he regards the denomination she leads as false. He has stated publicly that the Roman Catholic Church possesses the only true Christian faith. His condemnation of the ordination of women bishops is an affront to every Christian denomination believing in the equality of women. It is a snub to the Anglican Synod and will earn the contempt of every fair-minded person. Frederico Lombardi, a Vatican spokesman, underscored how the ordination of women was "a crime against sacraments". It is salutary that impartiality has not been described as a crime against God. This it can never be. It is a very disturbing and unwelcome challenge to entrenched autocratic religionists. Like all other oligarchies clericalism will fade away wherever there is genuine freedom of conscience.

Property rights

I have already described the historical treatment of brides in Indian society and hinted at the kind of power that the custom of dowry exerts. It is within living memory in Britain that upon marriage a woman's total property passed to her husband. It was not until the passing of the

Married Women and Tortfeasors Act that brides were able to retain their property. Later legislation also ensured her entitlement to some of her husband's estate in the event of his predeceasing her or the marriage breaking down. Most pension schemes have built-in rights for widows' pensions (and widowers'!). The non-contributory Civil Service Pension Scheme has a compulsory 100 per cent contribution in respect of widows. In the event of a man remaining a bachelor there is a refund. It is not unknown for men to defer marriage until after retirement. I have mentioned primogeniture (where property devolves upon the eldest son) but not emphasised that such a system cut out women altogether when it came to the inheriting of land. In most cases of unmarried sexual relationships even of a longstanding nature a women has little recourse to law. In some instances if a woman can prove she contributed towards assets she can get recompense. In African custom such women are regarded as common-law wives and have more protection. It is not uncommon for wealthy women film actresses and multi-million-dollar heiresses to enter into pre-nuptial agreements or make special wills to keep their husbands from gaining any access to their fortunes. These ladies tend to marry several times in succession. It is like a gender reversal of King Henry VIII. In virtually all other cases wills written before marriage become invalid after it has taken place. This gives a bride, or bridegroom for that matter, relief from former bequests and promises, but it can be particularly disadvantageous to women in some circumstances.

A mixed status

The more genuinely democratic and more sophisticated a society becomes the greater the chance is that female equality with men will be more in evidence. The rule of law is a great stabiliser. On the other hand in more deprived and primitive societies, women continue to lose out. Slave trading has not been universally eliminated even though it is illegal. Across frontiers criminals are still able to exploit women in the sex trade especially when they are deceived into expecting a better life in a wealthier country. Even in such countries husbands abuse their wives and female partners to such an extent that secret refuges have to be provided for women and their children. At one stage in the United Kingdom a Child Protection Agency was set up in order to compel men who had left a wife and family to provide financial support. The system became unwieldy and practically unworkable. The real miscreants were seldom apprehended while those who had made initial handsome provision were made to pay all over again.

Social progress

There are other new social advantages for women throughout Europe. For instance there is statutory provision for paid maternity leave including in some cases leave for fathers to help out. Major firms make provision for crèches for children and offered staggered-hours work contracts. There are tribunals that adjudicate and sometimes compensate when there are allegations of sex discrimination in the workplace. There is more protection and understanding of the position of women in the armed forces.

An Equalities and Human Rights Commission has been in existence in Britain for some time. It is headed by a man and it is currently in turmoil. Laws on discrimination are being updated. A radical new Equality Bill is due to be enacted in 2010. It will amount to a huge consolidation of nine existing laws and a large number of statutory instruments relating to race relations and amending and simplifying the Disability Discrimination Act of 2005.

It is one thing to enact laws and quite another to enforce them. There is greater willingness on the part of employers to prevent discrimination arising in the first place through education and training schemes. Councils, police forces and hospitals will be required to report on gender pay and private companies with more than 259 employees will be obliged to follow suit by 2013.

Ground to make up

According to *GEO; Allen & Overy:*

- Women earn, on average, twenty-two per cent less than men.
- Disabled people are more than twice as likely to be out of work as non-disabled people.
- People from ethnic minorities are thirteen per cent less likely to find work than others.
- The average equal pay claim takes seven years to be resolved.

- Without change, the pay gap will not close until 2085 and it will
- take almost one hundred years for ethnic minorities to get the same job prospects as others.

According to Cassandra Jardine:

- 75 per cent of childcare during the week and 66 per cent at weekends is done by women.
- 8.1 per cent of directors of banks in the FTSE are women.
- 19 per cent of our MPs are female.
- 16.4 per cent is the average pay gap between men and women working full-time in the UK.
- 30,000 women lose their jobs every year because of pregnancy.
- 89 per cent of carers are women.

Chapter Fifteen

CONTEMPORARY SCENE

> "Seeing the multitudes Jesus had compassion on them. They were harassed and distressed and were like sheep without a shepherd." Matthew 9:36

Wolves and sheep

This is the most difficult chapter I have ever had to write. I will be critical of attitudes. However, I am not setting out to single out individuals. There are so many people of different creeds and of different degrees of enlightenment or lack of it: so many of them with real callings and vocations. There are some who are sincere, follow tamely what they are taught, and do not think for themselves. However, not many out of all these conjecture whether a leader is a wolf in sheep's clothing. How often is it asked who the people are that are like sheep without a shepherd? This was a potent saying of Jesus intended to warn believers and cause them to identify false teachers. This was not a reference to some abstract and distant situation. It refers to our own doorsteps just as much as it did to the Sanhedrin. The relevance of these remarks to women is that they have been suffering as sheep without caring shepherds for centuries. Of course, some women can operate as wolves as well as men. There are she wolves. Before I reveal what is at the heart of the suppression of women in the Church I am going to deal with some different women and the ways in which these ministered. My full reason for so doing will become clearer in my closing chapters where I describe the priesthood of all believers and do not shirk facing up to both the dangers and joys of entering into the full liberty with which Christ has made us free. I am listing eight women of recent times, four of whom were humble servants of Christ and four others who were, in some respects, exhibitionists. I am not including instances of exhibitionism to bring women into disrepute as some do, but because this information is relevant to my case for women. My purpose is to set these alongside some outstanding women servants of God. According to the Bible we should be prepared to judge all things spiritually. It has nothing to do with gender. It would be just as easy for me to provide lists of men. We must leave it to God to judge people. However, unless actions and motives are judged there is always a danger that wrong priorities will be followed and in some cases personalities will be emulated. There is a warning here to over-ambitious women. And to everybody who sows to the flesh. However, all of these women preached the gospel and it should be remembered that the apostle Paul was glad whenever the gospel was preached even if it was out of ambition, or of strife, or of envy (Philippians 1:15-18). A contemporary problem that is wider than the context of this book but relevant to the following examples is extremes of belief. At one extreme are those who have a form of godliness but deny its power and at the other there are those who, instead of waiting for the real power of God either resort to pretence or else look to other sources both psychological and counterfeit. Thankfully in the middle there are many balanced believers.

Which are the most faithful servants?

Mary Slessor of Calabar, Nigeria, served as a missionary and teacher in Nigeria for thirty-eight years. I have already referred to the deep respect for this woman across all the tribes. Many of the early leaders of the country, when it achieved independence from colonial rule, had been educated at her school in the South East. She made no claims to supernatural powers: the love of Christ just shone out of her. She understood that to strive to be fully like Christ (to be conformed to his image) was to serve others in His vineyard. Her great work amongst Nigerian mothers and their children served to lay sound foundations in society as did her exposing of witchdoctors and occult practitioners. She was the very antithesis of a proud person and never worked up emotional situations.

Aimee Semple McPherson was a Pentecostal preacher, something that, basically, was a welcome acknowledgement of the concept of equality of women in the Church. However, she is reported by secular writers as having covered up an affair by claiming to have been abducted and abandoned in the Mexican desert. She was married three times. She drew thousands not so much by preaching but by claims of divine healing, and freezing in one position in a trance. She followed Woodworth-Etter as a practitioner of "slaying in the spirit", something passed on and still being indulged in by fringe charismatics. What is the point of it? She died of an overdose of sleeping pills.

Amy Carmichael of Donavar, a young girl in Northern Ireland, besought God for a long time to give her blue eyes like her contemporaries. She also sensed a call to the mission field. It was only when she went to India that she realised brown eyes were much more acceptable and understood that God had known best. Amy's exploits in India are a legend. She founded a huge and flourishing work. After some years of active service she injured her back and became bedridden. She then founded an extraordinary intercessory ministry. She endured years of pain with great patience.

Maria Woodworth-Etter followed Aimee Semple McPherson and emulated her but went to greater extremes. Maria would freeze for twenty-four hours when thousands of people came to gaze upon her. She was a self-declared prophetess who said, untruthfully, that the San Francisco Bay area would be destroyed by an earthquake and a tidal wave in 1890. She was an early practitioner of the slain in the spirit phenomenon. She was happy to speak in Mormon churches.

Isobel Kuhn was for many years a great missionary worker amongst the Lisu tribes in Chinese provinces. It is heart-warming to read of how many of these people became staunch believers and persevered under persecution. This was tough, arduous, and challenging service. It started from the time of leaving Bible college where she married, and later had a joint ministry with her husband. She returned home to America with terminal cancer and over a period of five years wrote a number of bestselling books about her experiences. These were brilliantly written and inspiring works.

Kathryn Kuhlman, originally a devotee of Aimee, became world-famous. There was much that was arresting about her ministry. Her critics, and there were many of them, helpfully exposed her shortcomings without mentioning what was puzzling. I will deal with what was doubtful first. Dr D Martyn Lloyd Jones, the greatest preacher of the twentieth century, was a distinguished physician before entering Christian ministry.

In a booklet he gave an assessment of the healing side of Kuhlman's ministry. There were medically confirmed healings, unlike some of those that are commonly reported today with no medical backing. The doctor faced up to this, but was unwilling to attest that these were of a divine origin. Her meetings were highly theatrical and she dressed like a film star. She had a worldly and extravagant lifestyle. Her house was packed with costly antiques. A prominent male evangelist had his career cut short when he divorced his wife to marry Kathryn. She lost her "power" and then divorced him to get it back again. There is evidence that towards the end of her life she lost the "power" which seems to have consisted of slaying people in the spirit. She had a number of male adherents who achieved prominence in the realm of psychic phenomena. For instance one of them stood on her grave in order to get power from her bones!

Gladys Aylward failed an interview with a missionary society and had the extraordinary faith to catch a train through Siberia to China at her own expense to join a little work. The Inn of the Sixth Happiness was a rest house for travelling traders. It was a Chinese custom that guests were told stories before retiring for the night. Gladys was able to introduce Bible stories. She encountered hostility from the local mandarin but when the Japanese invaded China he was so impressed by her witness and her endeavours to stop the practice of female foot-binding that he became a Christian. She led a large group of children through mountains and across a river to escape the enemy. She brought them to safety. It is notable that after returning to England her exploits were turned into a film. She was so self-deprecating that some over-pious ladies' fellowships took her off their list of speakers.

Agnes Sandford was instrumental in bringing aspects of New Age thought into the Christian Church. The main problem with her teaching was that she believed it was possible to "intuit" angels. Because of people's susceptibility there was a large increase of angel sightings following her ministry. Biblically, angels are messengers sent by God for a purpose. There is no way that we should sit down and imagine their presence.

Only one class of Christian

According to the Bible there is now only one class of Christian. Both men and women are kings and priests to God and are ordained to bring forth fruit. With maturity, some will be endowed with ministry gifts but all should have a burden for the lost. Jesus Christ, the Son of God, in a body, observed all the people around him and said they were like sheep without a shepherd. Yet there was a temple, there were feasts and ordinances, a High Priest, an Aaronic priesthood, and a Sanhedrin. There is a great lesson in this for us today. Jesus stated, further, that the religious authorities were teaching according to the traditions and doctrines of men. He was not one to find fault and do nothing about it. He brought about the abolition of the letter of the law and replaced it with something better: grace – His Father's plan of redemption and a new birth.

The Bible is absolutely clear that Jesus is now the one Great High Priest: minister of a heavenly tabernacle that God has pitched and not man. There is no longer any need for sacrifices, because one great sacrifice was offered on the cross. There is no longer any need for priests to stand daily offering ceremonial sacrifices. The reintroduction of a sacrificing priesthood and two separate orders of Christians (clergy and laity) was the result of man-made policy. The imposition of a superior caste of male clergy with claims of supernatural sacramental powers was the means of subjugating the masses and denying women equal rights in the Church. In fact, man-made religion is a bad witness to society. It has resulted, particularly, in the unjust exclusion of women, quite apart from its dogmatic behaviour towards all believers throughout history. (See Appendices at end.)

The idea of a wolf in sheep's clothing is that the wolf is not immediately apparent, especially when his outward appearance gives an impression of piety and beneficence. Paul declared himself to be the chief of sinners, so how can orthodoxy justify its claims to individual holiness. Only God is holy. The Catholic catechism states that the Church is holy because it teaches a holy doctrine. The Church only stopped putting people to death when it lost temporal power. How holy is the selling of "holy water", the doctrine of indulgences, auricular confession, and the subjugation of women? Jesus said that nobody is good save God. We are all sinners saved by grace so it is audacious to hold oneself out to be "His Holiness". There is only one kind of Christian: one that is born again of the Holy Spirit. That is what Jesus told a Jewish religious leader.

The opposition

In the latter part of the last century after considerable debate women were ordained in the Church of England following the Ordination of Women as Priests Measure in 1992. This was not accepted by numbers of male clergy. So much so that some defected to Rome and were told by Cardinal Hume that they must "accept the whole menu". Those who complied must have had a terrible antipathy towards women. Others sought to exclude ordained women from certain dioceses or requested to be given special peripatetic bishops. I have mentioned elsewhere, and answered, the objection that Jesus only chose men. Another dubious orthodox assertion is that its doctrine of apostolic succession of men is a bar to women. There is neither credible proof nor Biblical authority for such a succession. This was admitted by a leading Catholic archbishop who wrote *Catholic Apologetics* (Archbishop Sheehan). What about the claim that Jesus only called men? Good lateral thinking will allow that it would have been improper for an unmarried Jesus to issue a direct invitation to a woman. Many women did follow him spontaneously, and he was glad that they did. The mud-slinging was bad enough. Jesus was criticised for speaking to a Samaritan woman, allowing a sinner woman to wash his feet, being a wine bibber, and having a devil. Present-day fantasists say that Jesus married Mary Magdalene. What was the ground for an apostolic succession? That when a papal delegate stated that Pope Celestine was a successor of Peter nobody contradicted him!

A current controversy raises the question of whether women should be bishops. So fraught are Anglican relationships that a fair sized contingent of bishops refused to attend a Lambeth conference and chose to meet instead in Jerusalem. They constituted a forum called GAFCOM. Strangely these men represented both ends of a theological spectrum: High Church and Evangelical. They also had a double agenda: objecting to women in the ministry and objecting to the ordination of gay and lesbian clergy. One might well question why they do not question other aspects of each other's theology and how far, in the case of their objection to women, they are afraid of a probable threat to their promotion prospects.

Some years ago I used a homely and cheap hotel near Church House, Westminster. It was during a train strike. I found myself having breakfast with twelve clergymen. Not one of them spoke to me, not one of them gave thanks, but all of them talked all the time about pay scales, increments, and pay increases. They were a bunch of professionals. One of John Stott's curates launched a book (*As It Was In The Beginning*) at Southwark Cathedral and I bought two copies. The prebendary (who was reported to be a spiritualist) said, "You seem to believe it." The author of that book is now a Greek Orthodox bishop, believing in the authenticity of icons!

As far as objection to the ordination of gay and lesbian clergy is concerned, my book is not about this. In passing, however, GAFCOM and a newer group, the Fellowship of Confessing Anglicans, would accept celibate homosexuals because they see nothing unscriptural about this. There are Biblical grounds for the limitation and why they should go no further. I believe this is still the view of Lambeth. It is becoming too "politically correct" when people are admonished for holding to this view, and I cannot see logically how it can be said to offend the human rights of others. The right of free speech is an important human right as well. Society has made many changes in its attitude towards active homosexuality. Active homosexuality is no longer a criminal offence if practised between consenting adults. However, personal disagreement with this ought not to result in police interrogation. If someone expresses an opinion that the intended biological gender differences of men and women were for the natural procreation of the human race, and contends that without such a difference the world would not be populated it should be respected. It is one thing to legalise a behaviour and quite another thing to gag people because they do not agree with it.

To return to my subject, the opposition of these two groups to the creation of women bishops is on the grounds that women ought not to anoint. A function of a bishop is to anoint in the ecclesiastical processes of confirmation and ordination. If Jesus Christ, the Son of God, was content to allow two different women on separate occasions to anoint him then that is good enough for me.

Women bishops

In July (2009) the Synod of the Church of England decided to initiate a process ending in the ordination of women as bishops. This disturbed a number of male clergy who have organised groups to fight against a satisfactory final outcome. They hope to raise theological arguments that will throw the process off course. They claim to have conducted a furious re-examination of scripture and I have already refuted their findings. Their laborious argument that the Greek word *kephale* means *head* is a storm in a teacup. The word is only used to described man's traditional role in the family and not his standing before God in spiritual things.

They argue that every word that Paul wrote should be on tablets of stone although Paul made it clear that only some of his advice was received directly from the Lord. They respect women and think they are honouring them by using the word of God to exclude them. They separate worth from power. I have already contended that claims to sacramental power are man-made. The word eucharist was not used in the early Church nor does it appear in the Bible. Transubstantiation was not part of Roman thinking until 1215 AD and was influenced by Thomas Aquinas who said that Jesus confirmed this to him by speaking to him from a crucifix. He also claimed that Peter and James came back from the dead to talk to him in his room. I have taken this information from Catholic books. I do not wish to offend Catholic friends. I am only raising this issue in defence of women who are being excluded from what are man-made traditions. A careful study of the sixth chapter of John's Gospel and the Book of Leviticus will prove that Jesus was speaking spiritually and not literally when he instituted a breaking of bread and drinking of wine as a remembrance of his approaching death. The evangelicals in GAFCOM should take particular heed of what I have written and consider whether their opposition to women's rights ought to be well down their list of priorities by comparison with the damage that their orthodox bedfellows are doing to Christians' rights to be taught a true gospel that will give them a full assurance of faith.

Another objection to women bishops is that women should not have overall administration of dioceses. They are worried that this is about to happen. What is their problem? They just do not want to surrender an entrenched position. They argue further that if women are given equal rights that within twenty or thirty years society will be profoundly confused about sexuality and gender. It is more the case that for the past one thousand years or more society has been hoodwinked into believing that God is not impartial. They ask how it will be possible for young people to learn God's beautiful pattern of family life. They even suggest that the ordination of women will cause people to lose trust in the Lord. Having made such emotive comments they go on to equate the ordination of women with the error of building tower blocks in inner cities! As to the orthodox members of GAFCOM, I would like to ask these why they do not say more about the destruction of family life and of faith of those who have been abused by "celibate" paedophile priests in vast numbers. It is possible that future woman bishops would not cover up serious abuses to the same extent than has been allowed by male bishops in their dioceses in the past. One cannot imagine women transferring paedophiles to some other parish so that they can perpetrate their bestial practices upon even more unsuspecting children and families. However this is only an opinion.

A more compelling argument than boosting the virtues of women *en bloc* is the plain fact that men have nothing to boast about: nothing to justify a claim of superiority.

Now this is a scandal that has rocked the world. America, Australia, the United Kingdom, and the Republic of Ireland. As an example, a report has just been published entitled *The Report of the Dublin Archdiocese Commission to Inquire into Child Abuse.* It alleges sexual abuse of 450 children in the diocese of Dublin alone. Earlier the Ryan Commission Report found systematic sexual, physical and emotional abuse of hundreds of thousands of children in institutions run by The Christian Brothers, Sisters of Mercy, and other religious orders. Dr Diarmuid Martin, the Archbishop of Dublin, has said that since 1940 more than 400 children had been abused by at least 152 priests in the Dublin area, and the horror of that abuse was not recognised for what it was. He told his congregation the report's revelations would shock and horrify everybody. He went on to say that it was likely that thousands of young people were abused by priests in the period under investigation.

The commission was established in 2006 and has investigated how allegations of child sex abuse made against a representative sample of forty-six priests were handled by nineteen bishops in Dublin from January 1975 to April 2004. The report is likely to produce evidence of how bishops sought to cover up activities of paedophile priests by moving them from diocese to diocese, thereby facilitating the abuse of children over a wider area. The arrest in 1994 of Father Brendan Smyth, who was convicted of abusing children in Dublin, Belfast and the USA over forty years led to the collapse of the Irish government. Last year Cardinal Desmond Connell, who was replaced in 2004, abandoned a lengthy challenge to his successor's transfer of tens of thousands of Church files to the commission. The cardinal, who retired under criticism for his handling of clerical sex abuse allegations, argued that the files were legally privileged. The commission investigated nineteen bishops, seven of whom are dead. Its report is expected to name fifteen priests, eleven of whom have already been convicted.

In addition to the scandal of paedophilia alone there is, in addition, an attendant story of cover-up by bishops. This has arisen on account of the godlike character built around the priesthood. Men with such fabricated supernatural powers are regarded as untouchable by the hierarchy. Repentance has to be dragged out of them.

I have found it distasteful to write about paedophile priests and evasive bishops, as I am sure countless decent Catholics will in having to read about the subject. It is unavoidable, in making a case for women bishops, to air these evil happenings for consideration by GAFCOM and one of their spokespersons, the Vicar of Christchurch, Westbourne, Bournemouth. How can he possibly assert, in the light of the preceding paragraphs, that "women bishops would have a more adverse affect on people's faith or their beautiful pattern of family life than men" when men not only cover up paedophile activities but allow them to spread by sending evil priests, under a cloak of anonymity to another parish. His allegation that a woman bishop is not suitable for cross-parish management looks positively ridiculous in the wake of these scandals, and the number of educated women in the Church. Looking at this situation objectively it is not necessary to elevate women by claiming they are superior just because they are of a different sex. They are just entitled to be treated impartially as human beings. In the face of events men's claim to superiority looks very thin. Women could hardly do worse. These remarks are, of course, only applicable to regenerate people. Jesus said that, "Anyone who harmed children would be better off if he had a millstone hanged round his neck and was cast into the sea." Bear in mind that under Roman law in Jesus' day one could be tied into a sack with a snake and thrown into the sea for being unable to repay a debt. Whoever heard of a paedophile who repented?

Women objecting to women

I am reproducing below a letter sent to a leading national newspaper by a woman in order to show how it is possible for people to be misled by religious doctrine and tradition and so become opinionated.

> I am surprised that a priest does not understand that those of us who are unable to accept Communion consecrated by a woman are not concerned that she is unworthy. Nor are we faced with making an individual choice over the matter.
>
> We believe that the Church of England is part of the universal Church and that the Synod had no authority to amend 2,000 years of Christian doctrine. We accepted this doctrine when we were prepared for confirmation but are now required to renounce it to fall in line with secular trends.

> We believe that, worthy or not, women have not been validly ordained and so such sacraments are not valid.
>
> In the Church where I regularly worship there is a retired ordained woman who is universally liked and respected; if it were a matter of personal choice I would find her more acceptable than any male priests I have encountered, but on rare occasions when she is celebrant a group of us are obliged to worship elsewhere, not in protest, but in order to receive the sacrament.

I trust that this book has gone a long way towards opening the eyes of religiously indoctrinated Christians. The letter writer has correctly identified her beliefs as resting upon 2,000 years of Christian doctrine. She presumably means the long ladder of ever-changing dogmas that comprise the basis of her religiosity and not the faith once delivered to the saints. (See Appendix 2.) Just the same as she fails to recognise the validity of a woman's ordination so, the validity of her male priests is not recognised by Pope Benedict XVI. She need not worry because the idea of a consecrated sacrificing priesthood is stated to be obsolete in the Book of Hebrews. The word "sacrament" does not appear in the Bible. Confirmation as conducted in the Church of England can be a blessing because, together with the instruction preceding it, there can be a deepening of faith. However, I see it as no more than a ritualising of spirit baptism. Just as a priest cannot in God's eyes automatically baptise a baby and say he makes it a child of God, neither can a bishop "confirm" people unless it strengthens them with His power in the inner person. It is not uncommon for an unsaved bishop to confirm an unsaved person in his or her sins.

This letter confirms my contention that a major objection to the ordination of women is based on belief in a sacramental system. This is something that the evangelical component of GAFCOM ought to sort out. Christianity is, broadly, so mixed up that some so-called evangelical leaders, especially the Anglicans, are halfway towards Rome at heart. There is a book, whether dishonest or ignorant I will not judge, called *Growing into Union.* It presents Roman Catholicism as what it is not. Now Roman Catholics are quite unequivocal about their main tenets and should be respected for it. So why did the authors and a body called ARCIC (Anglican Roman Catholic International Commission) misstate so much about it. (See Appendix 3.) Was it for the purpose of selling it as more palatable to the average Anglican? Why did prominent Anglicans subscribe to it? They were running with the hounds and riding with the horses. I suspect that at heart they liked the autocracy and the subjugation of women. These are the people that are prepared to join forces with those who preach another gospel, which is not a gospel, as a price for keeping women outside: women who are fellow heirs of the Kingdom of God. For the benefit of readers who are not familiar with the differences between the theologies of the Eucharist expounded by Rome and by Anglicans I have added an Appendix 3 to this book. My sole purpose in doing this is to show that the Roman doctrines of sacraments and sacramentals hindered the emancipation of women in the Church because the administration of these was kept as a male prerogative.

The fact that Romanism has infiltrated the Anglican Church has contributed to a hardened attitude against women by some. This is substantiated by defections to Rome whenever measures are put in place to advance feminine liberation.

PART III

THE QUICKENING SPIRIT

A Synthesis: The chapters of Part III consist of a summary of my case for the absolute rights of women in the Church and of changes that might occur and, if realised, how far these would result in fuller experiences of liberty in the Holy Spirit. If the trappings of tradition and ceremony, poor substitutes for the power of the Holy Spirit, are stripped off it will open a way for greater corporate participation in service and worship. All men and women would become more effective kings and priests to God. ***I emphasise that Part III does not relate to non-spiritual aspects of the case and seeks not to be judgmental of these.***

As to a summary: imagine that counsels have made their replies: the Judge has pondered, ruminated, and then finally spoken as follows:

> "The case" refers to an argument often put forward by men that women do not have the same rights as them in the service of God. Men, by teaching, imply that God is not impartial in his treatment of women. They say that He too believes women are inferior. A counter contention is that men are wrong and misrepresent God's perfect will. God has always exercised utter impartially and is devoid of favouritism. He makes all who receive Christ new creatures, and this is why women should never be treated as inferior to men in His service. It follows from this that sections of the visible Church are in error when adopting discriminatory practices. Radical steps must be taken to rectify this long-standing injustice. These changes are likely to result in leadership problems but useful lessons can be learned from instances in the past when others sought to bring about such changes as this. Complete perfection cannot be expected in the present dispensation, so does this mean that some interim degree of accommodation will be necessary? If this is so, what then is a tolerable minimum acceptable level of compromise? Unity in love is a precious thing and must not be lost by giving more weight to less important factors. The history of denominationalism is littered with divisions over things that could have been lived with. If Catholic theologians had acted over faith and works like Peter and Paul did over Gentile inclusion, reformation could have been achieved without fragmentation. Luther was undoubtedly right to say about justification by faith: "Here I Stand." (Peter had all the authority but he was the one who gave way.) Those with authority were

proud and stubborn and instituted a "counter reformation". Are those in authority today also too proud to give way? Are intellect and self-interest to remain handicaps as well as, in the case of intellect, an aid when used wisely. Jesus said, "It is the spirit that quickens – the flesh profits nothing." Paul wrote, "God has quickened us together with Christ (by grace you are saved)."

Chapter Sixteen

THE UNCHANGING GOD

> "Jesus Christ the same yesterday, today and forever." Hebrews 13:8

> Great is Thy faithfulness, O God my Father,
> There is no shadow of turning with Thee;
> Thou changest not, Thy compassions, they fail not;
> As Thou hast been Thou forever will be.

The Spirit and the Flesh

None is perfect or holy in his or her own right and all are susceptible to new-fangled ideas. Only God is perfect, holy and unchanging. God's dealing with us is on an entirely spiritual basis. After all God is a spirit. It follows that acceptable management of the true Church depends upon the adoption of and adherence to spiritual precepts. There should be no room for man-organised religion. The Bible states that when the Lord Jesus ascended on high He took captivity captive and He gave gifts for individuals. These were of both ministerial and spiritual kinds. These were set in the Church from the outset by God Himself and are described in Ephesians 4:11-13, and 1 Corinthians 12:7-11. Their purpose was to equip members for effective service and worship. So, for example, pastors, evangelists and teachers were intended to bring all the rest to a required and God-pleasing standard. Unfortunately, whenever the spirit departs its power is substituted with symbols, ritual and autocratic systems. God's teaching is hijacked and usurpers wrongly reinterpret this in order to give themselves power. This is in spite of the Lord's declaration that leaders should not lord it over people as the kings of the Gentiles did. The following inalienable rights have fallen victim to the traditions of men: impartial treatment of women, universal acceptance of the purity of God's precious word, and the supernatural power of God.

In the beginning

One problem with Bible expositors is that they do not, generally, excel in lateral thinking. They stay too close to an immediate scripture. This may be the reason why Jesus said on one occasion that the children of this world would be wiser in their generation than the children of light. God does not change nor does His wisdom: this has resulted in Him allowing that mankind will fall below His expectations and need to be afforded a certain amount of latitude. He has endured the contradiction of sinners against Himself in a process of reconciliation aimed ultimately at changing mortal beings for the better. In the beginning Adam and Eve were innocent, they were vegetarian and so were animals. There was an open opportunity for creation to remain unchanging and eternal. One day there will be restoration and a renewal even better than Eden but it will be beyond our history. The existing creation is not totally depraved, as some extremists assert, but it is, sadly, far short of the glory of God. It is fallen. It can be convicted by the Holy Spirit and those who are transformed into the children of light should act as salt as part of their reasonable service in the Kingdom of God.

Be you perfect as your Heavenly Father is perfect

Perfection is only a goal. The present world is imperfect and is unlikely to improve as it follows its prince and decent people depend upon themselves to improve. Even believers will struggle with their old selves. As to their new nature, the Christ life, Jesus Christ likened Himself to a corn of wheat that fell into the ground so that it did not abide alone but brought forth much fruit. The fruit of the spirit of life in Christ that should be brought forth by those who sow to the spirit is love, joy, peace, patience, gentleness, goodness, faith, meekness, and temperance. Change is wrought by God and opposed to works of the old self which when sown produces contrary behaviour: this stretches from selfishness and greed to malice and murder. All those who are in Christ partake of the divine nature. (The Church is indebted to Bishop E W Bullinger,

DD for his classic writing – *The Two Natures in the Child of God.)* The Apostle Paul was able to state: "I (that is self) am crucified with Christ. It is no longer I that live but Christ that lives in me. The life I now live I live by the faith of the Son of God who loved me and gave himself up to death on my behalf." It must never be overlooked that the law was Paul's schoolmaster that brought him to Christ. It was good but it did not give him power to obey it. He was unable to fulfil the law in his own strength. He could do all things only through Christ who strengthened him.

That which is entirely perfect will only be achieved by ransomed souls at the second coming of Jesus or, individually, when each is called home. Heaven is perfect. When the appointed numbers have entered, the last trumpet will sound and the dead in Christ will rise and be changed. And God will wipe away all tears from their eyes. There will be no more death, neither sorrow, nor crying, neither will there be any more pain, for the former things are passed away. There will no more be any marrying or giving in marriage because bodies will be spiritual and glorified. God will dwell with His people. Gender will be of no consequence.

Ideally, God would wish that things were perfect now in this world but this can never be the case. In eternity God will put his laws into people's hearts, and they will not teach everyone their neighbour, saying, "Know the Lord": for all will know him, from the least to the greatest. Down here we are dependent upon his word and those who teach it faithfully and accurately. Unfortunately, Jesus found that there were those, who when they taught, were in need of being taught themselves. A gross example is that of teachers who fail to recognise the right of women to be equal with men in spiritual matters.

What hinders

There are many hindrances to the emancipation of women in the Church. These have already been identified elsewhere, but a summary is as follows:

1. **Failure to realise that an unchanging God has unchanging standards.** Therefore, standards of spirituality must embody His character and cannot be changed. Whatever is tolerated by way of accommodation in the form of tradition, culture, and custom must not be allowed to affect people's true spiritual standing before God's holy presence. Everyone who is born of woman is looked upon impartially by God. He is no respecter

of persons. Everyone who is born again of water and the Holy Spirit should be led by the spirit and be equally impartial. There are no scriptures that authorise male ascendancy in spiritual matters: rather there are many that indicate God's impartiality as to gender in this realm. It is a mistake to equate earthly tradition with God's standards for his Church.

2. **Failure to come to terms with rebellion.** The main cause of rebellion is to get one's own way and consequently gain advantage over others. This grew from an individual advantage contrived by Cain by killing Abel to subsequent corporate conspiracies conceived in tribalism, nationalism, and religion. It is not implied that tribalism, nationalism and religion are entirely wrong. There are within them many elements providing protection and a sense of belonging. These are better than total non-belief. It is just that whenever these become instruments of suppression they fly in the face of a perfect God. We should love the Lord our God with our whole heart, mind, and soul, and our neighbours as ourselves. In fact Jesus loved us more than himself. The word of God should not come out from us: it should come unto us only. In other words, every time we put our own brand and mark upon it there will be a fallen motive of making people follow us to our own advantage. "I am of Paul. I am of Apollos." The strongest objectors to the appointment of women bishops are male bishops. They are advocates in their own cause.

3. **Narrow views of scripture.** Scripture is the inspired word of God and every word included in it is true. It does not follow that every action recorded in it is pleasing to God. The slaughters by Jehu and to a lesser extent by David certainly were not. Outside of the Ten Commandments a lot of the law was expanded by Moses and allowed by God, as a dispensation, until something better emerged. Jesus did not go out of his way to attack the concepts of foreign gods or temporal governments but He disagreed strongly with a backslidden Judaism. The fact that Paul wrote certain things does not mean they should be taken out of context or beyond what was intended. Moreover, character faults, such as Peter's, do not detract from the word of God, but rather serve to convince people of its authenticity and honesty. Psalm 137 describes those men as happy who seize infants and dash them against the rocks. How can this verse be taken as something God would approve of? Clearly, as the Bible states, "The prophets are subject to the spirit of the prophets." In fact, Jesus

taught against taking revenge saying, "You have heard it said an eye for an eye, and a tooth for a tooth: but I say unto you, that you resist not evil: but whosoever shall smite you on your right cheek, turn to him the other also." There are two lessons to be learnt here. Firstly Psalm 137 is a challenge to sharpen one's perception. The Son of God was at variance with this stark statement. Many people find it difficult to understand that such a bald statement is meant to challenge our perception of right and wrong. Conversely, many others find it difficult to live up to sublime teachings in the Sermon on the Mount. But how many face up to this or anguish about it? Inability does not negate the challenge or mean that we should not want to rise to it.

Religious tradition

There is a great deal about Christian orthodoxy that is an adapted and perpetuated form of Judaism. It also appropriated to itself religious forms to create a self-empowered "monopoly". Thus the Catholic Mass is said to be the sacrifice of the new law whereby Jesus is offered continually on the altar in an "unbloody manner" through the ministry of his priests. These priests are exclusively male and it is claimed that they are a privileged and superior class of Christian. Scripture states unequivocally that the one sacrifice of Jesus is sufficient for all time and that there is no need for priests to stand continually offering sacrifices anymore. Yet the Catholic Mass by a contrived misinterpretation of scripture is said to be the place of literally changing bread and wine into the body and blood of Christ to be adored and administered as an efficacious means of grace.

When Jesus said that except people ate his flesh and drank his blood they had no life in them (that is eternal life), many left him because they were aware of the teaching in the Book of Leviticus that blood is not to be drunk. Hence the Jews only eat kosher meat to this day. So taking his disciples aside, Jesus explained that the Spirit gives life and the flesh counts for nothing. It was the words which he spoke that were Spirit and life. There was nothing literal about his statement. On another occasion Jesus fell out with Pharisees and other teachers of the law for their insistence on ceremonial washings and proscribing of certain foods as unclean. Jesus said these were but rules taught by men. They nullified the word of God by their tradition. Nothing outside of a man could make him unclean by going into him (or clean either). It is what comes out of man that makes him unclean. Earthly food does not go into a man's heart but into his stomach and then out of his body. What comes out of men's hearts such as evil thoughts, sexual immorality, theft, murder, adultery, greed, malice, deceit, envy, slander, arrogance and folly are evidence of an unclean nature.

It was thought necessary to confront the whole question of the Eucharist, not with a view to offending people's opinions, but because it has been a prime cause of woman's subjugation in the Church. It has always been declared as a male prerogative: a monopolistic male power. It is proclaimed as a power coming from an unbroken line of male bishops. Its Biblical legitimacy has been queried by knowledgeable nonconformists. The footnotes in the Catholic Jerusalem Bible already referred to incorrectly imply that what evangelicals regard as a Bible-based breaking of bread service is false. If the writer of this allegation had a balanced understanding of the scriptures he would have seen just how precious and central the early Church's breaking of bread was. In Acts 2:42-47 it states that they devoted themselves to the apostles' teaching and to the fellowship of breaking of bread and to prayer. Everyone was filled with awe, and many wonders and miraculous signs were done by the apostles… . They broke bread in their homes and ate together with glad and sincere hearts, praising God and enjoying the favour of all the people. It was a snide accusation to take an honest account of poor behaviour in one place in order to replace the teaching of Jesus with a symbolic Roman Mass that reduces Jesus to a wafer and imprisons this emblem in a metal tabernacle. If this seems harsh then people in glass houses should not throw stones especially when the exclusion of women is involved.

In order to avoid partiality the case dealt fully with the propensity of some evangelical ministers to wrest single scriptures in order to justify the authority of men over women. These ministers fail to distinguish between male authority arising from tradition, culture and custom and female right to spiritual authority in the presence of an unchanging God. The New International Version wrongly translates Paul's views as "teachings" at the beginning of the eleventh chapter of first Corinthians. In the original it is made clear that he was describing tradition or ordinances. They should review their position before God. If adverse comments are thought by traditionalists to be confrontational then they should allow that their own unequivocal assertions merit an equally strong response.

Spiritual blindness

Such blindness results in refusal to repent of the dismal failure to bring about the unity that Jesus prayed for. It also gives rise to the spiritual deceit of misquoting God in order to exploit, deceive, and spiritually damage ordinary people. Jesus said of some religious men that they did not enter the Kingdom of Heaven themselves and prevented others from going in. How do they do this? By teaching wrong means of entering into life. This gives people false assurance and prevents them from seeking the truth of the gospel. Repentance towards God and faith in the Lord Jesus Christ and belief in His death and resurrection is the simple truth. It does not matter whether it is a man or a woman who explains this. Any other way, especially one with "magical" elements or with a requirement of life-long self-effort, is a cruel bondage and not the liberty wherein Christ makes His people free.

Understanding. It is not right to condemn individuals: rather one must seek to understand them. Say rather, "there but for the grace of God go I". Do not equate Rome with Babylon or the Pope with the anti-Christ as extreme Protestants have done. However, it is right to entreat others to take stock and examine themselves to see whether they be in the faith or only partly in it. This was added because there is much about Catholicism that is rooted in truth. One can subscribe to the Apostles' Creed and be thankful for the preservation of knowledge of the virgin birth: if not Mariolatry. Before Constantine imported superstition and violence, the early Church combated many gross heresies. Later those who held to scripture were wrongly branded by this Church as being the heretics. Ordinary people did not stand a chance of understanding how truth was running away from them. They were like sheep without a true shepherd. Women were subjugated.

Men should change

God does not change. He has no need to. There is plenty of scope for men to change. The face of Christianity could change for the better overnight by a process of simple decision-making. There are sections of the broad universal Christian Church that acknowledged the spiritual equality of women from the time of their institution. Others had the wisdom to introduce such a freedom along the way. Some may be imperfect in other respects, but then there is no such thing as a perfect church on earth. The Salvation Army, Pentecostal Churches, Methodists, some Baptist Churches, some independent Free Churches, and many missionary societies do not discriminate against women. Apologies are due to those who have been left out. Of course, there is an ongoing debate within the Anglican Church and, hopefully, those who oppose the ordination and further elevation of women will see sense, or else they will be out-voted.

The Hand of God

It has been shown how God patiently brought His people on a long journey from the times of Abraham to what was called "the fullness of time". This was when he sent His Son to redeem them. It is clear that the structure of things moved from personal faith to the law: from a large and complex religion to, eventually, a handful of isolated believers. At this point they were of one mind, heart and soul. The miraculous was an open event. Whatever happened to spoil this happy situation? How is the hand of God to be seen in the way things have worked out up until this day?

Temporal power and persecution

Whenever the Church was in temporal ascendancy or allied to secular powers it failed miserably. Whenever it was persecuted by the world it triumphed gloriously. God's greatest lesson was the seeming curse of the cross of Christ: the greatest failure in the eyes of the worldly, and the greatest wonder to those with an eye of faith.

Signs and wonders

Jesus foresaw the danger of signs and wonders on demand. A wicked and adulterous generation would only be given the sign of Jonah (a guarded reference to his own death and resurrection in three days): only Naaman was healed of leprosy when there were many lepers in Israel. If the miraculous was seen as salvation by the unbeliever it could prevent repentance and newness of life in the spirit. Today it is all too evident that, for some, experiences of charismata have become the be-all and end-all of their spiritual quest. This is wrong. But it is equally wrong to deny the prospective presence of the power of the Spirit today and that God still sets ministry gifts in the Church; desires his people to seek spiritual gifts; and wishes them to worship Him in spirit and in truth.

Lessons

It is against this background that churches must prayerfully consider what the will of God is as to their priorities. They must neither quench the Spirit nor grieve Him. The greater priority: a need for a changed life, is discussed in the next chapter.

CHAPTER SEVENTEEN

RIGHTEOUSNESS A KEY

> "The Kingdom of God is not meat and drink but righteousness, and peace, and joy in the Holy Spirit." Romans 14.17

The key

The case is that men and women are regarded as equal in the Church when they are "in Christ". In other words they are equal when they are made righteous by God. It follows that people are not necessarily righteous on account of belonging to a denomination or attending a particular church or having charismatic gifts. It is the spirit of life in Christ that gives newness of life and freedom from sin and death. There is a translation out of darkness. Peace and joy in the Holy Spirit stem from partaking of the divine nature. Peace and joy are two of the fruits of the spirit of life in Christ listed in the fifth chapter of Paul's letter to the Galatians. (There is a separate list of gifts of the Holy Spirit in the twelfth chapter of Paul's first letter to the Corinthians.)

God's righteousness

The greatest emphasis must be placed upon the need to prioritise the truth of a present spiritual Kingdom of God on earth because those who are Christ's are (present tense) translated out of darkness by the Father into the kingdom of His dear Son. It is the kingdom and not the visible church that embodies righteousness. It is critical to the case that neither men nor women are good or evil on account of their gender. Whatever good is displayed by anyone is as a result of a righteousness given by

God. This limits the membership of the true Church. In other words a real or authentic Christian is identifiable by the life and not by membership of a denomination or church. The true Church is sometimes said to be an invisible one. Tares are sown among the wheat. Bishop J. C Ryle has left us with a classic definition in *The True Church Along These Lines.*

A present kingdom

This kingdom is not of a tangible or material nature. That is why it cannot be shaken. It should be the instrument of unity but, regrettably, it is regarded as being of minor importance by comparison with other doctrines. In this kingdom it should never be conceded that women do not have the same spiritual rights as men. This kingdom was imminent in the ministries of John the Baptist and the Lord Jesus. It broke into history at the death and with the resurrection of Christ. As the curtain in the temple was miraculously riven apart, the event symbolised the end of all partition. All were one in Christ. The Israel of God was established on earth as an enclave of the one eternal kingdom.

Work in the kingdom

A primary work in the kingdom is that of evangelisation and witness. Women have proved their prowess and effectiveness in spreading the gospel. On far-flung mission fields nobody challenges their right to equality. This is because there is comparatively little earthly reward, it is dangerous, and shortages of callings mean that men do not feel threatened.

Another work is that of mercy; a means of winning souls by exercising love in the form of practical help and material provision. If one has saving faith then works will follow. Women are particularly suitable helpers in caring for the sick and dying and getting alongside poor families. Their work is accepted per se but seldom afforded sufficient accolades to achieve parity with men in ordained ministry. An assertion by a spokesperson of GAFCOM that women are not competent to manage more than one parish is an absurdity. There was Deborah, and in society we have women prime ministers, women monarchs, women high court judges, women academics, and they do very good jobs.

Entry into the Kingdom

When a religious man came to Jesus by night, Jesus told him that he must be born again. Jesus was surprised that a religious leader did not know this and added that without such an experience one could neither see nor enter the Kingdom of God. It follows that all who enter this kingdom are made new creatures in Christ and that those who do not enter are still in darkness. Both men and women enter this kingdom on the basis of being made righteous. God's expectation is of obedience, openness, and honesty. Once it is seen that this kingdom only contains one class of citizen and does not recognise any super-significance in buildings, symbols and ordinances it is much easier to realise that its principles are based on utter impartiality.

Faith of the Kingdom

Both men and women exercise saving faith. There is also a spiritual gift of faith given to people in exceptional circumstances. It is evidenced particularly on the mission field and in countries where there is persecution on account of being a follower of Jesus. Surely there are not teachers who dare to suggest that spiritual gifts are exclusively for men. So why should ministry gifts of the Spirit be regarded as compartmentalised so as to exclude women from being apostles, evangelists, pastors and teachers? They should not! It has been shown already that a sacrificing priesthood is obsolete and invalid. Its introduction led to the artificial institution of two classes of believer. A realisation of this removes from intelligent debate a major part of the case being made by men against women's ministry. In order to avoid misapprehension about genuine leadership it is acknowledged that God sets in the Church the ministry gifts noted above. It is up to Him whether to call a man or a woman. But gifts are given not for the purpose of lording it over the others. Those who serve should reckon themselves as the least. Their wonderful privilege is to build up their equal brothers and sisters in Christ until they all come in the unity of the faith to the measure of the stature of the fullness of Christ.

Prayer of the Kingdom

Jesus uttered two particularly poignant prayers. The first has come to be known as the Lord's Prayer or "Our Father". It was a wonderfully impromptu prayer from a divine mind. It was given, interestingly, as an example of how to pray. It has become a repetitive prayer especially when recited as part of the rosary. Jesus did not favour repetitive prayer because it would become too automatic and less from the heart. A boy was given the saying of ten "Our Fathers" as a penance and lost count when in the course of recitation. Jesus framed the Lord's Prayer at a time when the Kingdom of Heaven was still imminent or at hand. Therefore the words, "Thy kingdom come" were a total truism. The words apply today in the sense that we should pray for an advance of the kingdom on earth and can apply to the coming visible kingdom in the future as at the end of Revelation. "Maranatha: Our Lord Come." If prayed, however, in the context of the present earthly spiritual kingdom and acted upon it could become a great basis of unity. This would not just be a unity of man. This potential unity embodied in the Lord's Prayer was perceived by Dr D Martyn Lloyd Jones in his exposition of the Sermon on the Mount, and by Pope John Paul II in his private diaries.

A second prayer was uttered just before Jesus went to the garden of Gethsemane, and is recorded in the seventeenth chapter of John's gospel. Again, there is an emphasis upon unity: that, we may be one, even as He, Jesus and the Father are one. Here the unity is by an indwelling, "Thou in me, and I in them". The mystery hidden from the ages is Christ in us the hope of glory. It was also a revelation of the source of eternal life. Jesus has been given power over all flesh. Eternal life is in knowing; The Father, the only true God, and Jesus Christ whom He has sent. He finished the work. He was about to go to the cross. The indwelling Christ is for whosoever will come to Him.

We do not always know what to pray for as we ought. It is part of the ministry of the Holy Spirit to help our infirmities by making intercession for us with groaning that cannot be uttered. It is a splendid means of avoiding self-indulgence and mis-praying. A defect in some churches is a lack of support for prayer meetings. Is this because people have not learnt to pray? Is it because of prayer bores? Or are many people not very close to God? It has already been shared what a hindrance it was when men only were allowed to pray.

The Kingdom and the word

Jesus overcame Satan purely by quoting the word of God which is the sword of the Spirit. "Man cannot live by bread alone but by every word that proceeds out of the mouth of God". The case for the freedom of women in the Church rests upon scripture and no other reason is either permissible or necessary. Faith comes by hearing the word. They that hear the word of Jesus and believe in the one who sent him shall not come into condemnation but have passed from death to life.

An adversary

Satan is an adversary of the kingdom and of women in particular. He is an adversary fighting against righteousness. Paul writes about the fiery darts of the "most wicked one". He goes about like a roaring lion seeking whom he may devour. He is so high in the angelic order that we cannot rebuke him. We must say, "The Lord rebuke you, Satan." If we resist the devil he will flee from us. Mentioning the evil one has been avoided until now because it is too easy to blame him for every evil. He can be used as a false excuse for our own wayward actions.

It is plain that this unpleasant enemy of our souls is opposed to women. Genesis 3.15 states that God put enmity between Satan and the woman. It was the seed of a woman (Mary) that crushed his head. It is argued that God is not pleased with the antipathy shown against women in the Church. It is now stated boldly that nobody is more pleased than Satan at such a state of affairs. It means that family prayers are hindered, that men do not recognise that women are equal fellow heirs of the present spiritual kingdom of God. Women cannot contribute to their full potential in public prayer and worship. A prayer to deliver us from evil because the kingdom is God's is a confirmation that light and darkness are opposed in a present earthly conflict.

As far as religious professors are concerned, the word has questioned that if the light that is within them is darkness, then how great is that darkness. When Satan is thrown into the abyss perfection will abound. When Satan is released from the abyss he will be confronted by resurrected saints who will by then be completely conformed to the image of God's Son. It will not be a return match with a fallen Adam and Eve but with a new creation. For example, in that creation Adam and Eve will not be like they were in their fallen state: they will be like Jesus was when he overcame the temptation of Satan in the wilderness. Neither will they, in glorified bodies, be treated differently by God on account of gender.

Doing the right thing

Doing the right thing is being honest and loving. It is being fair and impartial. It is not an act of selfishly preferring oneself over others. What a difference it would make to our greedy society if everyone could be like this. What a difference it would make to the Church if everyone could be like this. What a difference it would make to witnessing if everyone could be like this.

Also if men are generous with their wives and do not withhold earnings unfairly to indulge their own lifestyles, interests, and amusements, then there would be more money available for the poor and the Lord's work. Then the Lord would open the windows of heaven, and pour out a blessing, that there is not room enough to receive it.

Finally, there is the awful quandary about omissions. What have we neglected to do? What wrong priorities have we adopted? Who has lost out on account of our lack of care? Do we all go our own way too often? Answering these questions will make us more tender and susceptible to God's perfect will. It may convict some of their ambivalence in the matter of feminine emancipation in the Church.

A gift

Righteousness is not an inherent quality but a gift of God. The mistake of Israel was of being ignorant of God's righteousness. They went about to establish their own righteousness. The history of the Christian Church is littered with failures due to man's self-righteousness. The story of the two men who went to the Temple to pray is a wonderful example of what I am writing about. The first man blew his own trumpet. The second man confessed his sinfulness and went home more justified than the first man. It is a fault whenever men proclaim that they are superior to women. In fact, because righteousness is a gift of God nobody can claim any merit for being washed by the precious blood of Christ. When Paul made this point he also mentioned those who were still unrighteous and went on to say, "And such were some of you."

Witness

If we love our neighbour then we will want to win him or her. There is no better witness to others than leading a righteous life. Jesus taught that we should so let our light shine before people that they may see our good works and glorify our Father who is in heaven. These works, of course, are the result of imputed righteousness and are not of ourselves unless we should boast: they are foreordained. That is the guaranteed outcome of those who walk after the spirit.

Many ordinary people today are worried at the lack of moral teaching in schools and society generally. They are beginning to realise that youngsters are getting out of control. There is no longer the teaching of Sunday school and the difference between right and wrong. It is righteousness that exalts a nation. Conversely, an unrighteous nation will not flourish. The eyes of the Lord are over the righteous. A few righteous people would have saved Sodom and Gomorrah. The sin of Sodom was not committed by women. Women were abused there.

A woman can have a big influence upon her family especially if she has Christian principles. Many women are estranged from organised Christianity because they are not accepted as equals. Who can be more undiscerning than the GAFCOM vicar, already cited, who claimed that a woman did not have the ability to run more than one church? It is a poor witness to those without when Church leaders glorify themselves; when they become political; and when they order people about. People will follow a good shepherd but not sheep shearers. The shepherd who loves Jesus will feed His sheep. He will not discriminate.

Chapter Eighteen

KINGS AND PRIESTS TO GOD

> "And (Jesus Christ) has made us kings and priests unto God and His Father." Revelation 1:6

A true ordination

Jesus ordains his followers, both men and women, to go forth and bear fruit. In this capacity they are both kings and priests. They are kings to serve and priests to worship. One can study any number of scriptures relating to kinghood and priesthood and none of these offers any opportunity of being read as applying to men only. These all relate to every believer. Let us look at some of these scriptures:

1 Peter: 2 and 9: "You, as lively stones, are built up a spiritual house, an holy priesthood to offer up spiritual sacrifices acceptable to God by Jesus Christ. You are a chosen generation, a royal priesthood, a holy nation, a peculiar people; that you should show forth the praises of him who has called you out of darkness into his marvellous light." Here Peter is addressing the whole Church and attributing kingly (royal) and priestly functions to all who have been redeemed. These scriptures are backed up in **Hebrews 13: 15, 16,** in which sacrifice, praise and thanks are the fruit of the believers' lips and of their reasonable service including doing others good. These two offices of king and priest are mentioned again three times in the Book of Revelation. **Revelation 1:6, 5:10, and 20:6.** These scriptures show the two offices operating firstly as a present fact, secondly at the second coming of the Lord Jesus Christ, and thirdly during the millennium. This shows how appropriate the exhortation given by Peter of "continually" proved to be. On the basis of the unchanging spiritual character of God's kingdom all these scriptures must apply to men and women equally.

Tensions

There is no difficulty in visualising the harmony, peace and unison that there will be in eternity both in worship and in service. Conversely, there are tensions when it comes to showing how this perfect unity can work out on earth. It helps our understanding to draw on problems that have arisen due to change in the past. Paul laid down a lot of teaching about conducting worship in a corporate way and it can be assumed that this was the pattern adopted by the early apostolic Church. One can see that things did not always work out, particularly at Corinth.

The nature of things was that when people came together everyone had a psalm, a doctrine, a tongue, a revelation, an interpretation. They edified one another by prophesying. All could prophesy according to the measure of their faith. It was not revelatory. It follows that they conducted a breaking of bread, studied the apostles' doctrine and prayed. We know that on at least one occasion the breaking of bread became so disorderly, that at times everyone spoke in tongues at once, and that too many people prophesied. Some women were talking at the wrong time. There may have been a woman who was telling people what to do when she was insufficiently instructed. Paul established guidelines to help. For example prophesying should be limited to two or three, people should not all speak in tongues at once, and not speak in tongues at all unless there was an interpreter.

In England in the nineteenth century a Presbyterian minister, Edward Irving (1792-1834), formed a sect that sought, amongst other things, to get back to apostolic ways. He was, initially, very respected. (However, he mistakenly supposed that the orthodox system of seven sacraments was apostolic.) Long before the advent of modern Pentecostalism he sought to reintroduce the operation of inspirational gifts into public worship. Two lady members of his church thought that their human imaginations were, in fact, gifts of the Holy Spirit and very quickly their folly was made manifest. The sect went into a steep decline. The Bible exposes those who say "God says", when he does not. It was a sorry episode that foreshadowed a continuing problem.

How then does one discern between genuine spiritual manifestations and what is imagination and counterfeit? The Bible has a lot to say about false manifestations. These can hinder what is true and are ignored by those "who want something to happen", without waiting upon God. There is the genuine power of God which must be waited upon; there is human imagination; there is hysteria; and there is counterfeit power. Many sincere Christians are not prepared to accept that at the present time there is an upsurge of hysteria. They are, understandably, so anxious to see God at work that they are undisciplined and so oblivious to counterfeit manifestations such as the so-called "Toronto blessing". Others make a mistake by opposing the real power of God on the grounds of excesses like this.

Importance of the Lord's Supper

The following questions are intended as a challenge. The ritualistic nature of the orthodox Eucharist has been challenged already, and here the question relates to the manner in which other churches conduct the breaking of bread. It is usually a periodic short appendage to a service and in most cases gives little time for reflection or awe. There is fear or reluctance on the part of ministers to allow spontaneous prayer or participative worship. Such decisions are understandable because of the "empty vessel syndrome". However, there should be a desire for greater openness and liberty in the Holy Spirit and also for wisdom to ensure there will be suitable control. The problem in the medieval Church was that the Holy Spirit left it in the same manner as His glory left the Jewish Temple. It was then deemed necessary to resort to ritualism. It was not possible to will the Spirit's presence or as David Wilkerson put it, "to conjure up the Holy Spirit".

In spite of known problems it is clear from the Bible that God likes more than a one-man-band. Therefore, surely it is better to allow greater freedom but with awareness and caution because God is not the author of confusion. He does not like control freaks either. A thriving Baptist Church began to experience more of the power of the Spirit from the leadership down. People were taught about inspirational gifts. So nervous was the oversight that, if someone had a revelation they had to whisper in the pastor's ear. He then either approved or disapproved. If he cleared it the person was free to speak to the Church. Where is this in the scripture? Again it is possible to sympathise with the dilemma. However, a reason for its cause may have been that too many believers are reluctant to leave their present comfort zones.

So what is being suggested? God's ideal is that believers should exercise kingly and priestly functions. Under such orchestration ordinary men and women would have a freedom and liberty in worship. However, things have not worked out at all smoothly in cases where churches have sought to follow a back-to-the-Bible approach of such a kind. However, why should present modes of service remain just as they are? Are churches quenching the spirit? Where is their present vision leading them?

Progress

For a start there should be a desire, if not a complete activation, of measuring up fully to God's purposes: a readiness to wait on empowerment. There is nothing at all to prevent a complete acceptance of a policy of gender impartiality. This would be like a great breath of fresh air sweeping through the Church. It could lead to much blessing because God is pleased with obedience and not with ceremony and ritualism. Complete parity could, theoretically, be introduced at once. This could be regardless of any other changes contended for because it is the main burden of this case. Assuming that real Christians are being addressed, the next priority might be to ask the Father for the power of the Holy Spirit. Revival comes with godly repentance. The Bible states that the best gifts of the Spirit should be coveted and there should be recognition that ministry gifts are more than intellectual ability and theological training, although the latter is a great complementary factor in being strengthened by the spirit in the inner person. The understanding and the Spirit are inseparable companions. One problem is that intellectual Christians who have not been gifted by the Spirit are unwilling to accept that gifts are for today. This is really because they have not experienced them. They become cessationists who hide behind dubious interpretations of scripture to justify a lukewarm position. The Bible states inspirational gifts will cease "when that which is perfect has come". This is weakly argued to be the completion of the canon of scripture, the death of the last apostle, or the consolidation of the Church. The life of John Bunyan serves to show how a comparatively uneducated and ordinary man could out-preach and out-write all the learned men of his day. This is a testimony to the continuance of God's power and to the fact that the Bible's reference was to the ultimate perfection at the end of history and to nothing else. When Dr Lloyd Jones was criticised for preaching a need for post-conversion Holy Spirit power and was told that all Christians received everything at conversion he looked at their dryness and said, "Really? But where is the evidence of this?"

In those churches that have made progress in the genuine things of the spirit, as opposed to emotional enthusiasms, it is suggested that attention is given to accompanying scriptures about the need for discernment, judgment, and the possible presence of false prophets. There is reluctance in many quarters to face up to the fullness of scriptural teaching about the need to exercise judgment. When two of the sons of Aaron offered strange fire, they were consumed by fire. I can only assume, after allowing that God is not unnecessarily vengeful, they had eaten some of the sacrifice and so did not offer it all up. Since under that dispensation the sacrifice was supposed to be whole burnt, I think the food illicitly taken burnt up as well. It is not ideal to surreptitiously introduce new spiritual experiences to a coterie in a church. There should be transparency and openness to everyone.

Quite innocently people today read about certain gifts and think they can appropriate or choose one. So a tap is turned on at eleven o'clock on Sunday mornings. The Bible tells us to wait on our ministry. Jesus said that there were many lepers in Israel in Elisha's day but only Naaman was healed. People then tried to throw Jesus over a cliff! On the other hand when even was come the sick were brought to him and he healed them all. This is not contradictory. It is a matter of being right with God. Healing is not a front-runner and Jesus was concerned much more about repentance and the overriding importance of rescuing people's souls. However, the instruction of James that the sick should send for the elders of the Church should be obeyed. The duties of a pastor include intercession that the Lord of the harvest will send reapers. The whole purpose of power is not exhibitionism or self-glorification but effectiveness in telling others the story. One can be confident that God's primary purposes will be served best when both men and women can be equal yoke-bearers in carrying out his great commission, and in doing so seek to worship him in Spirit and in truth – for he is seeking such!

Chapter Nineteen

GOD IS A SPIRIT

> "But the hour cometh, and now is, when the true worshippers shall worship the Father in spirit and in truth: for the Father seeketh such to worship him." John 4:23

From tent to tent

You have been conducted on a long journey. This has seen a spiritual progression starting from God's re-approach to mankind through Abraham, enduring the contradiction of sinners against Himself; the sending of His Son; the gift of the Holy Spirit, and a continuum of His battle against darkness. God's relationship with His people has shifted in emphasis from personal to corporate and back to personal. Religionists have resisted individual spiritual liberty all along. It was essential, as a growing-up process, that God chose a corporate nation, with which he could dwell. This period was dealt with in Chapters Eight and Nine. Part way through the latter there was a description of how the glory of God descended into the Holy Place. At that time God, who is a spirit, dwelt with his people Israel. It is important to remember that God does not change. We do and not always for the better. However, to those granted new life in Christ through the Holy Spirit ability is given to strive against the sinful nature.

There was a time when King David truly established his throne. David and the elders of Israel went to bring the ark of the covenant of the Lord from the house of Obed-edom with rejoicing to the city of David. And they set it inside the tent which David had pitched for it. Thanksgiving was sung. A loaf of bread was distributed to all Israel, both men and women. It is recorded in the seventh chapter of the Book of Chronicles that David was concerned because the ark resided in a tent while he lived in a house of cedar. He had in mind to build a house for the Lord and consulted Nathan the prophet.

God spoke to Nathan. David was not to build a house as God was content with the way in which He had gone from tent to tent from the day He led up Israel to the present.

A promised house

God promised that He would raise up one of David's offspring and establish a kingdom for him forever. He would build a house for God's indwelling presence. Many have taken this promise to apply to King Solomon, David's son who succeeded him, because he built a magnificent temple. Clearly they were not right. Yes, Solomon built a temple but his throne was not established forever. David was clear about this, recognising that God spoke about things that would not come to pass for a great while to come. He had been shown future generations. It is particularly wonderful that it was God Himself who was to build this house (1 Chronicles 17:25). The glory of God that came to the tent continued in the new temple until God became grieved by disobedience. His glory departed. There were successively two temples but neither was built by God.

The Messiah

The people of Israel were confident that God would send a Messiah although they, mistakenly, thought He would be an immediate earthly deliverer. This was especially thought to be so during the time of the Roman occupation: He would restore the kingdom to Israel. There had been so many predictions of a deliverer beginning with words directly from God immediately following the fall of Adam and Eve. Many subsequent great indications of a coming Messiah came through the prophets and these are familiar to many of us through lessons and carols read and sung during the time of Advent.

Reference was made to Malachi's sublime prophecy that the Messiah would come to the temple, and its fulfilment, in Chapter Three. It was related how Simeon and Anna each took the child Jesus in their arms and associated the promise with the moment. This fulfilment was a stronger proof that Jesus was the Messiah, as opposed to subsequent claimants, because the temple to which Jesus came was destroyed in AD 71, and there was no longer a temple in which another aspiring Messiah could appear.

John the Baptist fulfilled the prophecy of Isaiah as the voice of one crying in the wilderness to prepare the way of the Lord. The Lord Jesus was that Son of David who would build the true temple that God would pitch and not man. The apostle John wrote, "And the word was made flesh and dwelt ("tabernacled") amongst us, and we beheld his glory as of the only begotten of the Father full of grace and truth." As to the flesh he was great David's greater son: as to the spirit he was the Son of God.

Saviour and Redeemer

Jesus the Christ did not come into the world to condemn the world but that the world through Him might be saved: this was in a spiritual and personal sense. Firstly he suffered on the cross, the just for the unjust, to bring us to God. Secondly, the shedding of His precious blood, cleanses us from all sin and unrighteousness. A fallen humanity was redeemed from the curse of its initial disobedience. God threw a lifeline and it was up to people, individually, to grab hold of it. By repentance, working in them a Godly sorrow, they were redeemed. They were saved by God's grace. Religionists made a grave mistake in substituting this work of the Spirit with ordinances and symbols which they placed under their control. They made good works an additional condition of salvation despite the fact that God's word states, "not of works lest any man should boast". They failed to realise that God was a spirit and that it was His great plan that people should be indwelt with the Spirit of his Son, both men and women.

The hidden mystery

There was a mystery that was hidden from the ages up until the time of Christ. This was that the earthen vessel of the human body could be indwelt by the Spirit of Christ. "The mystery hid from the ages is Christ in us the hope of glory." This indwelling is described in a number of ways in the New Testament. In Chapter One, reference was made to Paul's letter to the Galatians in which he stated that God had sent the spirit of His Son into our hearts and showing that this included women. I do not think this is in dispute. There are other references in Ephesians, Colossians, Romans and 2nd Corinthians. The most telling is in the last great earthly prayer of Jesus recorded in the seventeenth chapter of John's gospel, "I in them".

The apostle Peter also referred to believers being partakers of the divine nature and this is a telling teaching because it distinguishes between life and power. The indwelling Christ-life is a result of the gift of righteousness. It brings forth fruit. The fruit of the spirit of life in Christ that frees us from the law of sin and death consists of all the attributes of goodness. This is a result of a new birth and it fits us for entry into the present kingdom.

The Holy Spirit

The Spirit of God, the Holy Spirit or the third person of the Godhead, is the divine activator who carries out or executes all the counsels and purposes of the Godhead. In creation the spirit of God moved upon the waters; in revelation it came upon the prophets; upon Sampson it came with might. In that the Holy Spirit came into the tent or upon persons He could also withdraw. There was never a guaranteed permanence. This is why King David prayed that the Holy Spirit might not be taken away from him. It is very important to note that David was not referring to his salvation. There is a distinct difference between life brought by the Holy Spirit and the power of the Holy Spirit equipping believers for service. Jesus said that it was expedient that he should go away (leave the earth) so that the Comforter (the Holy Spirit) would come and be the conveyor of new life. He would receive of the things of Christ and bring them to us. He would not glorify Himself.

Jesus as God in a body was confined to a location whereas the Holy Spirit would be omnipresent. The Spirit would convict people of sin, of judgment, and of righteousness. The Spirit's greatest work in God's plan was the conception of the Son in the Virgin Mary. In the same way the Spirit conveys the divine nature into believers' hearts at their conversion. Thus they are temples into which the Spirit of Christ can enter and dwell permanently. Paul wrote, "Know you not you are the temple of the living God." (1 Corinthians. 3:16) In Acts 7: 46, 47, 48, Stephen, a man full of the Holy Spirit and power, proclaimed that King David desired to find a tabernacle for the God of Jacob, but Solomon built him an house, howbeit the most High did not dwell in temples made with hands, as had previously been prophesied. No wonder that the Jews stoned him to death! It will disarm literalists today to state that God does not dwell in tabernacles made with hands. It is important to make this point because nobody should deny that women can know Christ in the heart and also receive the power of the Spirit. Those who rely too much on sacraments believe that a woman is born again automatically in physical water, baptism administered by a man, and that the Spirit is received at Confirmation and administered by a male bishop. These are automatic symbolic processes in which there is no guarantee of the Spirit's presence. This is not brought up in order to offend others who have every right to their own opinions. It is simply a contention that any views clashing with the word of God are based on man-made traditions and that these are invariably anti-feminist.

Fruit bearing

Jesus gave the perfect teaching of the complementary offices of the Father, the Son and the Holy Spirit. His father was the gardener, he was the vine and believers were the branches. To remain in him resulted in bringing forth much fruit. This teaching occupies the fifteenth chapter of John's gospel. The fourteenth and sixteenth chapters provide teaching by Jesus of the office of the Holy Spirit. The Spirit would not glorify himself but "bring glory to me by taking from what is mine and making it known to you". (16:14) What a clear picture this is of Christ as the first fruits and the Holy Spirit as the conveyor: the sap that runs along the branches of the vine.

The adversary

The progression of God's purpose for humanity is clear. Opposition comes from the Devil, the World, and the flesh. Christ overcame the Devil both in the desert and at the cross. However, this Devil is still the prince of this world and having lived for a great space of time is more experienced than any short-living mortal. He can be resisted by believers and he will flee from them. The world is far more seductive. The flesh (or the sinful nature), is a more dangerous adversary, and is opposed to the spirit even in believers. It has worked havoc even in the true Church whenever there was too much confidence in the flesh. This battle, however, is a personal or individualist thing. As individual temples of the spirit people are enjoined to come together as living stones built up together as a spiritual house for habitation by God the spirit. It was shown in the previous chapter that such a corporate outworking is fraught with difficulty for two reasons; the machinations of the Devil and sowing to the flesh.

The bottom line is the honesty of each person's relationship with God. When Jesus spoke to the Samaritan woman at the well he told her that Samaritans did not know what they were worshipping. He went on to say that the time would come when they would not worship God on the mountain they were on nor in Jerusalem. The time would come when they would worship God in spirit and in truth. That meant not in the temple of stone but on a personal basis in the complete liberty of human temples. Anything else that is of God in human earthly history can be reckoned as a bonus.

Knowing God

One can sympathise with the idea of monasticism without agreeing with it. The monk who retreated to his cell at every opportunity to commune with the Lord reckoned he was in a blessed state. He was free of the world, of the affairs of this life but he was not free of the Devil and his own flesh. Those who live in the world suffer all the diversions that the problems of survival create. Earning a living, bringing up a family, caring for others, are all legitimate preoccupations. But believers are saved to serve. The monk had more time to pray but friars were among the first to break out of the solitary mode.

It would have remained incredulous if the following statement had not been made by Jesus. It is both amazing and enthralling. Judas, not Iscariot, asked how Jesus would manifest himself to his followers and not to the world. Jesus answered that if people loved him, and kept his words; His Father would love them, and both He and the Father would make their abode with them. (John 14:22, 23) We know that all the fullness of God dwelt in Jesus. The epistle to the Ephesians embraces the pinnacle of spiritual experience which speaks of the glory of Christ's inheritance in the saints (saved ones). This is described as being filled with all the fullness of God. What a challenge to our faith!

A Spiritual Temple

In the twelfth chapter of Matthew's gospel, during a discussion about the Jewish Temple, Jesus stated that he was greater than the Temple. He spoke more positively after he cast the buyers and sellers out of the Temple. He said, "Destroy this Temple and in three days I will raise it up." The Jews, thinking he referred to the building, considered this to be impossible because it took forty-six years to construct it. But Jesus spoke of the temple of his body.

In John's vision of eternity there was no temple in the New Jerusalem: for the Lord God Almighty and the Lamb are the temple of it. There was no need of the sun and moon for God's glory lightened it. And so the progression is always from the finite to the infinite: from the corporate to the personal. The things that are seen are temporal and the things that are unseen are eternal. Failure of religious organisations cannot affect personal faithfulness. A spiritual kingdom cannot be shaken.

A challenge to faith

The reason for demonstrating a progression from the material to the spiritual, in the context of the title, is to indicate firstly the great difference between these two dimensions, and secondly to show that the case for impartiality as to gender rests powerfully upon our personal spiritual standing before an unchanging God. What pertains as to tradition, culture, and religious prejudice is symptomatic of the bondwoman. It can be said, as far as Christ's spiritual church is concerned, "Throw out the bondwoman." The bondwoman was born after the flesh; but the freewoman was by promise. These things are an allegory: for these are two covenants; the one from Mount Sinai which genders to bondage with her children and answers to Jerusalem that now is. But Jerusalem that is above is free and is the mother of all believers, both men and women. Paul finished these great thoughts written to the Galatians, for such they are, by exhorting believers to stand fast in the liberty wherewith Christ has made them free, and not to be entangled again with the yoke of bondage. This letter of Paul's was warning of the dangers of man-made religion.

The Power of the Spirit

There is a distinction between the fruits of the spirit of life in Christ which are the attributes of his divine nature (that is love, joy, peace, and so on) and the power of the Holy Spirit bringing ministry and spiritual gifts. Because God is looking for true worshippers to worship Him in spirit and truth it follows that this is the pattern that most pleases him. It is a pattern that fully accepts the equal rights of women in Christ. There is no reason at all why a woman should not be an apostle, prophet, pastor, teacher, evangelist or help. This brings the case to a vital and all-important point. There is total equality in Christ as between men and women. As to ministry and spiritual gifts, God sets these in the Church as he wills. It follows that in this realm it is a matter of calling rather than unquestionable equality: gender is immaterial. This is a pattern that is feared most by the Devil. That is why there are so many problems in giving liberty to all: problems that have been rehearsed. However, this does not mean we should shrink from seeking to be obedient and from coveting the best gifts.

Perplexities

The previous chapter reflected doubts about the true Church's ability to cope with spiritual fullness. Please pray fervently that it will. Whatever earthly outcomes as to worship and service there may be, we have a hope that is steadfast and certain. Jesus Christ is coming again, and then all striving will cease, because that which is perfect will have come.

The bright and morning star

Peter wrote about his great mountaintop experience when the Lord was transfigured and concluded that there was a more sure word of prophecy that should be given heed to. It was like a lamp shining in a dark place until the day dawns and the morning star rises in our hearts. This star was Jesus, the Messiah, who came out of Jacob according to the Book of Numbers, and which Jesus claimed for himself saying, "I am of the root and offspring of David and the bright and morning star." The morning star is an appropriate symbol with which to herald the second coming of Jesus and the revealing overtly of Christ's kingdom. The morning star can be seen with the rising of the dawn and be likened to the light that succeeds the darkness of this present age. Until then we have, in Christ, a great high priest, who has entered heaven itself. He is now the minister of the sanctuary, and of the true tabernacle, which God pitched, and not man. He is that tabernacle as shown in this chapter. He is the temple of the fullness of God, and all believers are kings and priests to God:

Christ the veil has entered,
With the blood He shed,
Sin's great debt is cancelled,
Love's own feast is spread:
Now in Christ we're chosen
Kings and Priests to be,
Living offerings bringing,
His own blood our plea.

(E C W Boulton)

The End

Appendix 1: Notes on Sikhism

Chapter Thirteen Sources

The Sikh Woman, G S Sidhu, 1977, The Sikh Missionary Society, UK, pages 3-12.

Sikhism & Guru Granth Sahib, S S Kohli, 1990, National Bookshop, Delhi, pages 86-91.

Punjabi Kinship & Marriage, Paul Hershman, 1981, Hindustan Publishing Corporation, India, pages 156-190.

Sikhism, Hew McLeod, 1977, Penquin Books, pages 241-250.

The Message of Sikhism, Harban Singh, 1978. Delhi Sikh Gurdwarg, Management Committee, pages 189-193.

Robber Noblemen, Joyce Pettigrew, 1975, Routledge & Kegan Paul, (this is a book about Sikh Jats – this caste is the largest of British Sikhs), pages 48-54.

Appendix 2: Calendar of Roman Tradition

Tradition was declared as of equal authority with the Bible at the Vatican Council of Trent in A.D. 1545. From 2nd century tradition has steadily led to an increasingly male dominated church. The following shows the years in which additions were declared as additions to Catholic doctrines:

1.	Presbyters first called "priests" by Lucian	2nd century
2.	Sacerdotal mass instituted by Cyprian	3nd century
3.	Prayers for the dead	AD 300
4.	Making the sign of the cross	AD 300
5.	Wax candles	AD 320
6.	Veneration of angels, dead saints, and images	AD 375
7.	Mass became a daily ritual	AD 394
8.	Beginning of exaltation of Mary. Term "Mother of God" first applied at the Council of Ephesus	AD 431
9.	Priests began to wear special clothing	AD 500
10.	Extreme Unction (rite for terminally ill)	AD 526
11.	The Doctrine of Purgatory by Gregory I	AD 593
12.	Latin used in worship	AD 600
13.	Prayers offered to Mary, dead saints and angels	AD 600
14.	First man declared to be Pope (Boniface III)	AD 610
15.	Kissing the Pope's feet	AD 709
16.	Temporal power of popes conferred by Pepin, King of the Franks	AD 750
17.	Veneration of the cross. Images and relics authorised	AD 786
18.	Holy water, mixed with a pinch of salt, chrism blessed by a priest	AD 850

19. Veneration of St Joseph AD 890
20. College of Cardinals began AD 927
21. Baptism of bells instituted by Pope John XIII AD 965
22. Canonisation of dead saints by Pope John XV AD 995
23. Fasting on Fridays and in Lent AD 998
24. The Mass gradually developed as a sacrifice, attendance made obligatory 11th century
25. Celibacy of priests declared AD 1079
26. Rosary adopted by Peter the Hermit AD 1090
27. The Inquisition instituted by the Council of Verona AD 1144
28. Sale of indulgences AD 1150
29. Seven sacraments defined by Peter Lombard AD 1215
30. Transubstantiation defined by Pope Innocent III AD 1215
31 Auricular confession (Rite of Reconciliation) of sins to a priest instead of God, instituted by Pope Innocent III AD 1215
32. Adoration of the wafer (called the host) decreed by Pope Honorius III AD 1220
33. Bible forbidden to laymen. Index of forbidden books AD 1229
34. Scapular invented by Simon Stock of England AD 1251
35. The cup forbidden to the laity at communion by the Council of Constance AD 1414
36. Purgatory proclaimed as a dogma by the Council of Florence AD 1439
37. Tradition declared equal with the Bible by the Council of Trent AD 1545
38. Apocryphal books added to Bible by the Council of Trent AD 1546
39. Creed of Pope Pius IV imposed in place of original AD 1560
40. Immaculate Conception of Mary proclaimed by Pope Pius IX AD 1854
41. Syllabus of Errors proclaimed by Pope Pius IX and ratified by Vatican Council (condemned freedom of religion, conscience, speech, press, scientific discoveries, and authority of rulers) AD 1864

42.	Infallibility of the Pope in faith and morals (Vatican Council)	AD 1870
43.	Assumption of Mary proclaimed by Pope Pius XII	AD 1950
44.	Mary proclaimed "Mother of the Church" Pope Paul VI	AD 1965

The argument is that "tradition" has always existed. It was handed down by word of mouth from generation to generation. This is not historically tenable.

Appendix 3: Differences in explaining the Eucharistic Rite

Roman Catholic Teaching	As represented by ARCIC
*The Holy Mass is one and the same Sacrifice with that of the cross, inasmuch as Christ, who offered Himself a bleeding victim on the cross to His Heavenly Father, continues to offer Himself in an unbloody manner on the altar through the ministry of His priests.	*It is possible to say at the same time that there is only one unrepeatable sacrifice in the historic sense but that the Eucharist is a sacrifice in the sacramental sense provided that it is not a repetition of the historic sacrifice.
*The sacrifice of the Mass is offered to Satisfy God for our sins.	*The Eucharist adds nothing to the efficacy of Christ's sacrifice on the cross.
*The Sacrament of the Holy Eucharist is the true body and blood of Jesus Christ, together with His soul and divinity under the appearances of bread and wine. The Blessed Eucharist is not a sacrament only it is also a sacrifice.	*The "real presence" does not involve a physical change. What is here affirmed is a "sacramental presence". The bread and wine become the "sacramental" body and blood of Christ.
Devout Catholics stand by these definitions.	These definitions are not accurate.

The Roman Catholic position is clear and most Catholics will stand by it. A joint body (the Anglican Roman Catholic International Commission) chose to misrepresent Catholic beliefs. Evidently the motive was to obscure what those actual beliefs were. The object might have been to soften the facts for Anglicans and the public at large, or to introduce Transubstantiation by the back door into the Church of England. It is noteworthy that in Greek mythology the mysteries were reserved for the initiated and the rest were not given full explanations.

Four Anglicans (two High Church and two "Evangelicals") wrote a book called *Growing Into Union* in which it was claimed that some difficulties were not real. For example they claimed some Evangelicals needed to be reminded that Catholics do not believe that they re-immolate Christ in the Eucharist or that the Eucharist is identical with His offering on the cross. This claim would astound most Catholics because their Order of the Mass states that, "The Divine Victim is immolated sacramentally".

The Anglican Series III Communion provides alternative wordings that can be adopted at the discretion of vicars according to whether they follow the Roman interpretation or hold an Evangelical position. Every ordained Anglican undertakes to uphold the Thirty Nine Articles. In reality this is not always regarded as a serious commitment.

Index

Index of People:

Referred to but not named in the Preface: